BIRTH OF THE BLUES
CHELSEA
THE FIRST DECADE

BIRTH OF THE BLUES
CHELSEA
THE FIRST DECADE
FROM THE RISING SUN TO THE OLD TRAFFORD CUP FINAL

BRIAN BELTON

First published in paperback 2008
by Pennant Books

Text copyright © 2008 Brian Belton

The moral right of the author has been asserted.

British Library Cataloguing-in-Publication Data:
A catalogue record for this book is available on request from
The British Library

ISBN 978-1-906015-24-4

Design & Typeset by Envy Design Ltd

Printed and bound in Great Britain by Creative Print & Design, Blaina, Wales

Pictures reproduced with kind permission of Getty Images and the author.

Pennant Books
A division of Pennant Publishing Ltd
PO Box 5675
London W1A 3FB

www.pennantbooks.com

CONTENTS

A PLAYER'S FOREWORD

BY PAT NEVIN (CHELSEA, 1983–88)

When studying history we want to know why the people who went before us behaved the way they did and if their actions had any lasting effects on those who followed them.

Certainly, we learn from this book that there are plenty of areas where the game, and Chelsea Football Club in particular, has had definite characteristics that have endured for an entire century.

Here we learn that even from before Chelsea's first introduction to League football there were complaints from other jealous clubs about the Blues buying success. From the first match at

Stamford Bridge, we also discover that the finances appeared as important as the club's scores to some observers. Maybe that was understandable because the wage bill was already a concern as the club had to find £75-10-00 (£75.50) every week to pay players and only had £162-13-01 (just over £162.15) in the bank.

I was pleased to discover that the Scottish links with the club were there at its inception but I hadn't realised that the tradition, so stoically upheld until the 1980s, of Scottish players getting drunk and behaving bawdily goes all the way back to 1906. The then player/secretary-manager Jock Robertson, found inebriated at the top of the stands wearing only long johns, hob-nailed boots and a bowler hat singing 'Scots Wha' Hae', was not the last from North of Hadrian's Wall to hit the Scotch at an inappropriate time around Stamford Bridge.

Even taking promising goalscorers like Frank Lampard from West Ham and making them into top-class players is mirrored in history with the tempting of George 'Gatling Gun' Hilsdon from Upton Park.

Here we find information about great players

from the very start of the club's history, including the heartbreaking stories of those who were called up to serve in the Great War, including Tommy Meehan who suffered terrible problems and Bob 'Pom Pom' Whiting who fell at Pas De Calais in 1917.

I was delighted also to read about VJ (Vivian) Woodward who is one man I am now going to personally find out much more about. An amateur and a gentleman, from what I have read about him here, he is someone who I can relate to maybe more than to any modern footballer with his ideological stance towards honour and fair play.

This book is a considered delve into the very early football and business history of the club and a must for fans in anoraks who need to know everything about Chelsea FC. It also contains much to interest the more casual fan sporting a replica shirt, even if it isn't a retro one.

A FAN'S FOREWORD

BY DANNY RIDGEWAY

The way forwards is backwards.

Dave Sexton (Chelsea manager, 1967–75)

I was born in Victoria, brought up in Chelsea, so they were my local team; there was no other choice – especially since my dad and two older brothers were already Chelsea fans. They took me to my first game when I was five against Blackpool at Stamford Bridge in 1961 – Chelsea won and the blue dye was cast.

It is difficult for people to imagine now but I had very little idea what to expect going to a football ground. It was the time before *Match of the Day* and 'wall-to-wall' live television. The only game on the telly was the Cup Final, but I can't even remember those games until the West Ham vs. Preston Final in 1964.

What I do remember is the crowds and the noise – nothing of the football, except that it was a long way off! At that time there was a dog track at Chelsea that surrounded the pitch, so for a small boy the players seemed to be miles away.

At school most kids supported Chelsea, although some supported Fulham and there were a handful of fans of other London clubs. I can't recall anyone supporting Manchester United or Liverpool, which is hard to imagine now.

It was easy supporting Chelsea because in the late 1960s and early 1970s most of my friends were Chelsea fans. We would all go into The Shed together and Chelsea had a half-decent team. Then, in 1972, the curse of Orient struck; 2–0 up and cruising into another Cup quarter-final and we ended up losing 3–2! A week later, we outplayed Stoke but lost 2–1 in the League Cup Final and it was all downhill from there.

Relegation!

I didn't understand the significance in 1961 but I certainly did in 1975, 1980 and 1988.

At times it wasn't easy being a socialist Chelsea fan during the dark, dark days of the anti-Semitics and racists who even booed our own black players. My response was: 'I was here before them and I'll be here after they have gone.' Thankfully, most of them have. Then there were the times like watching Chelsea lose 6–0 at Rotherham. The old guard that watch the glories the club now achieve can't help but look round and ask those who have joined the ranks since the coming of better fortunes how many of them would take that kind of disappointment for a season let alone seemingly interminable years.

I've still got season tickets and go with my sons and occasionally with my brothers if they are in London. But there is no doubt that the atmosphere has changed. The look you get when people hear that you are Chelsea fan: 'How many months have you been supporting them?' However, to be at Bolton with two of my sons when Frank scored those two goals in front of us was just bliss and no one can take that away.

If Roman gets bored with Chelsea and takes his money away, then I, like many others, will start supporting AFC Chelsea and the journey will begin again! The club got started over a hundred years ago with so much against it, so why not again if needs must? So, it might be a good idea for Brian Belton to write a book about just that subject – you never know, we might need a template one day!

Absent friends
The hardest thing about winning the League is those who suffered the years of rubbish and relegation but weren't with us to share it – my dad of course but also Gary Maguire who died aged 40 on 25 March 2004.

Gary was the quiz master for the away games and always kept us laughing on the long journeys back from yet another defeat.

Gary left his widow Mandy and two daughters, Megan and Holly.

Super Gary – A True Blue Diamond.

INTRODUCTION

In the whole long history of football, no club has rushed into fame with such sensational suddenness as Chelsea.

John Tait Robertson (Chelsea manager, 1905–06)

Chelsea Football Club is among the more unusual entities that make up the game's firmament. Historically, while their peers have been going in one direction, the esoteric Blues have often adopted an alternative course. The club are among the very few in the top flight of the game that took 'route one' into the elite echelons of football from their earliest days and this spirit has been something that has marked them out in the sport: an ability to move forward, with a mixture of finesse and fortitude in the face of doubt and at times condemnation.

What follows is an extraordinary story that could not be matched now or probably at any other point in history. Chelsea erupted out of the Victorian age into a new Edwardian era embodying a sense of renewal and promise that was characteristic of the time. The club was brought into being in a vibrant, young 20th century, wherein everything appeared to be possible for Britain and, in particular, at the very heart of its huge empire, London, one of the world's most powerful and wealthiest cities. Out of the buzzing and seemingly ever-growing metropolis, Gus Mears emerged, a product of an energetic epoch and a lineage of vivacious entrepreneurialism. His dynamic push had the capacity to enervate doubters and motivate those with imagination and ambition. He was one of those rare men that took ideas, visions and dreams and made them reality. Every inch a capitalist, Mears encompassed within that ethos the instinct to build a 'civil society' in which the duty to generate a 'civic' spirit is basic to the foundation of a society. This philosophy, premised on reciprocal duties and responsibilities, was a cultural instrument that was powered on the expectation that people might be able to work and prosper by their efforts and thus generate an environment that was 'convivial' and humane. To this extent Mears might be thought of as being a man made in the traditions of the Irish Whig Parliamentarian Edmund Burke (1729–97), and many of the principles voiced by that great statesman, political theorist and philosopher seem to suit the outlook Gus had, one very fitting declaration being: 'A disposition to preserve, and an ability to improve, taken together, would be my standard of a statesman.'

But, although Mears was the innovator, much more was needed to make Chelsea something that has endured for over a hundred years and become an entity that could transform, adapt and even at times resurrect itself. While chairmen and managers have provided the scaffold of the club, the soul of Chelsea has resided in the relationship between those who have played for the club and the supporters that have consistently made their way to Stamford Bridge to be part of a special collectiveness that is found in the practice of united hope that wants to make today a 'Blue Day' and for whom 'Blue is the colour'. The combination of and distance between defiance and desire, want and ownership provides the tension that makes for possibility, and that is what we live for – now, over thousands of games, more than a hundred seasons later, Chelsea remind their fans of this. What follows is the tale of the very start of it all, the 'Birth of the Blues'; from the time even before the idea of developing a professional football club in SW6 was first imagined to the Pensioners' first FA Cup Final. This was an epoch when the feeling that things could be done overrode the inane mutterings that would have it otherwise; a period imbued with the psychic and physical force to summon tangible worlds from the realm of dreams. The era was inhabited by people who saw it as their job, their life's work, to build the future from the raw material of inspiration.

Stamford Bridge arose out of the sands of the northwest bank of the Thames. That mighty construction held the prospect of embryonic tomorrows and from its great yawning womb a football team was born that would shake all the other great stadiums of the world, throwing a blue rainbow over the greatest game the world has known.

This book explores this time, the strength of will and passion and shows how its gift to history exploded into reality ... Chelsea, Chelsea; Chelsea, Chelsea ...

I will try to cram these paragraphs full of facts and give them a weight and shape no greater than that of a cloud of blue butterflies.

Brendan Gill (Writer for the *New Yorker*, 1967–97)

1
TAKE ME TO THE BRIDGE

In football, things are very unpredictable.

Gianluca Vialli (Chelsea, 1996–2000)

Unlike most clubs in the history of British football, Chelsea FC in effect arose out of their ground and Stamford Bridge has been the wellspring of the club's fate; the source of their fortunes as well as the threats to their very existence. But the great Blue chronicle would never have been forged into the vast library of Britain's sporting history if a huge, under-used and partly dilapidated piece of land had not been available and ripe for development at the turn of the 20th century.

In 1877, brothers James and William Waddell, a pair of former athletes and rich financiers, were freeholders of the plot where Chelsea's home ground would one day stand. The plot, which stood behind the Lillie Bridge sports ground, was originally part of an orchard and market garden, a place for the small-scale production of fruits, vegetables and flowers, which were often sold directly to consumers and restaurants.

The Waddell brothers purchased the land on behalf of the London Athletic Club (LAC) for £2,899 and built the first simple stadium as a base for the club who moved from their existing Lillie Bridge ground – their previous home from 1869 to 1877. The stadium was intended to provide a home for athletics in London as it was within a relatively easy journey from the centre of the city, and as such was seen as the ideal venue for competitors and spectators alike.

Stamford Bridge was opened on Sunday, 28 April 1877 with a crowd of around 6,000 in attendance. According to the *Fulham Chronicle*, 'Miss White, the daughter of the Lord Mayor, performed the opening ceremony, and there was a very notable gathering.'

THE BIRTH OF THE BLUES

The original Stamford Bridge ground had two stands, one on the east side and another in the southwest corner, both of which overlooked the running track, and, within a month of the opening, the first of many international athletic events had taken place.

The adjacent sports ground at Lillie Bridge had played host to the 1873 FA Cup Final between the Wanderers and Oxford University. Following their victory in the first-ever FA Cup Final in 1872, the Wanderers were allowed to defend the Cup in the second Final at their choice of venue, and, as they didn't have their own ground, they chose the relatively local Lillie Bridge. The modest 3,000 crowd – attributed to the Boat Race occurring later that day – saw the Wanderers defeat Oxford 2–0 to claim their second successive Cup Final victory.

In its heyday, in the Victorian area, the Lillie Bridge ground had a tradition of hosting hot-air balloon festivals and county fairs, as well as being the venue for a range of sports, including athletics and football; it had staged bicycle racing and hosted the first ever amateur boxing matches in 1867, the trophies for which were supplied by the Marquess of Queensberry. Middlesex County

Cricket Club moved to Lillie Bridge in 1869 but left three years later due to the poor quality of the turf.

The ground was the home of the Amateur Athletic Club which organised the Amateur Championships before they were taken over by the Amateur Athletic Association, and many world records were set at Lillie Bridge, including Marshall Brooks's 6' 2.5" high jump in 1876 in front of a crowd of 12,000.

From 1867 to 1887, Lillie Bridge hosted the annual athletics varsity match between Oxford and Cambridge Universities, which only transferred to Queen's Club on the ground's closure.

Lillie Bridge started to fall into disuse after the opening of Stamford Bridge and a riot (a mass act of hooliganism way before it became really fashionable) on 18 September 1887, which destroyed the track and grandstand. This was to be one of the final straws that finally forced the place to shut in 1888. The former Lillie Bridge ground, on Lillie Road, Fulham, London SW6, is now the site of a London Underground maintenance depot, Earls Court 2, part of the huge Earls Court Exhibition Centre complex, and the Empress State Building.

THE BIRTH OF THE BLUES

During August 1883, the Waddell brothers became embroiled in a financial crisis that led to their fleeing the country leaving debts of £30,000, an unfortunate consequence of which was the London Athletic Club finding itself £1,000 in the red!

However, John Stunt, a bootmaker who traded on the Strand in central London, who since the 1830s had owned a market garden, houses and stable buildings, which occupied about two and three-quarter acres next to the stadium, became the freeholder and secured its immediate future.

The London Athletic Club during the mid-Victorian period put Stamford Bridge to some very varied uses. Naturally, there were athletics events. This was a time when 'pedestrianism' was a fashion perhaps comparable to the height of the marathon-running craze of the 1980s and this was reflected in the pattern of usage. Arthur Wharton, England's first professional black footballer, smashed the world record for 100 yards in 1886 with his 10-second dash and my own great-grandfather, William Belton, competed in professional sprint races. William was to build a lasting relationship with the Bridge and was involved in training some

5

of Chelsea's first players, being hired by the club on a casual basis from time to time.

William had been employed in France to train with the fine Swiss middle-distance runners Paul Martin and Willy Schärer in their preparation for the 1924 Paris Olympics. The Americans Jackson Scholz, Charles Paddock and Horatio Fitch saw the positive effect of William's professional knowledge and took him on for a number of sessions. All this was a very risky business for the athletes. Although most of the top runners were taking 'unofficial' coaching at the era, it was strictly against the amateur code of the time. If the Games administrators had discovered that any athlete had trained with a professional, it would almost certainly have meant expulsion from the Olympics and probably from the amateur ranks. However, William's services were dispensed with, as Scholz (the Mississippi Cannon Ball) felt that constantly being beaten by the little feller was doing his morale no good.

In his time, William travelled throughout Europe, the USA and South America, spending his middle years training athletes, footballers and baseball players. When I was very young, it was my grandfather (William's son) who told me about my great-grandfather and the stories of the early Pensioners and the characters that populated Stamford Bridge in the first decade of the 20th century.

The Bridge also hosted corporate/company sports days where people ranging from civil servants to laundresses competed. These occasions were often grand affairs with a carnival ethos. Clowns, fire-eaters, jugglers, acrobats and stilt walkers made these events famous throughout London.

The diversity of events, even in the early days, seemed endless. In 1898, Stamford Bridge played host to the World Championship of shinty between Beauly Shinty Club and London Camanachd and in June 1900 there was a 'Highland gathering' at the Fulham Road stadium; the prizes were presented by the Marchioness of Tullibardine.

In November 1901, the Aero Club of Great Britain sent a balloon up to a height of 110,000 feet from the ground (it landed, relatively safely, in the Maidstone area). Sadly, tragedy struck at the stadium in 1902 when John Tickner dropped 100 feet to his death from the trailing rope of a balloon. Reverend John Bacon and his party had been competing in a race with a group of cyclists, and, once they alighted from the balloon, it had floated skywards again. Tickner, seemingly determined to prevent the huge contraption from escaping, was carried away. Those watching shouted at Tickner to let go of the balloon but he took this advice too late.

It was close to 20 years before any thought was given to the possibility that the stadium might act as a stage for regular competitive football. That vision was first mooted in a pub during a conversation between two brothers from the Mears family, Gus and JT. Both siblings were enthusiastic sportsmen and were particularly fond of football. Each had played the game and continued to take an interest in the sport after they hung up their boots.

Their builder father, Joseph Mears, was born in Hampshire in 1842. He married Charlotte in 1863, and their son Joseph Theophilus was born in 1871 followed by Henry Augustus in 1873. Joseph Mears senior died in the 1890s, leaving his sons financially well off, and by that time the Mears family were a well-known, long-established company of building contractors, one of London's wealthiest. Henry, known almost universally as 'Gus', continued in his father's business but he had a keenness for all sport. As a young man he had been a good skater and he went on to act as a judge at the Olympic Games and was chief marshal of the London Olympic marathon races, but football was always his passion.

A smartly dressed, square-shouldered, solidly built man with a thick moustache, Gus, together with his equally sports-minded brother JT, envisaged Stamford Bridge, close to the northern boundaries of Chelsea, becoming a centre of national and international sport. But it is their friend Frederick Parker who is credited with seeing the potential of a new stadium and understood to be the individual who came up with the idea to offer the Bridge as a venue for football matches.

The Mears brothers were accustomed to buying up land and property for redevelopment and resale and it was during 1896 that Gus in particular became enamoured with the notion of making Stamford Bridge a top football venue. So he approached John Stunt, who was loath to part with what was by now a prime piece of real estate. The Mears brothers would have known that a property boom would follow the Underground District Line extension to Putney Bridge, taking in Walham Green, which had been laid in March 1880, so their enthusiasm for the venture would not have been based solely on simplistic sporting philanthropy. Indeed, there was nothing in the Mears family make-up that would incline one to think that the brothers would go into any deal that wasn't underwritten with the profit motive. This was connected to the people they were and their entrepreneurial background and lineage; these were the times when such men believed that good business was the foundation of a healthy and wealthy society.

Stunt died in 1902 and Robert and Charlotte, his relations, began negotiations with Gus Mears in December 1902. The freehold of the stadium lands was transferred to Gus Mears on 29 September 1904, marking the start of 80 years of ownership by the Mears family.

There was, however, an impediment to the purchase of John Stunt's land, a clause in the lease stipulating that the London Athletic Club should remain the leaseholders for a stipulated period. This effectively dictated that athletics should continue on the purpose-built grounds for two years after Stunt's death. However, in October 1903, Mears acquired land previously owned by Stunt, part of it more market garden land, part no more than scrubby boondocks, which adjoined the stadium property.

JT Mears, by this point a speculator of some renown, was not a signatory of any documents to do with the site, but his connection to the venture is evidenced by the signature of Tom Lewin Kinton, JT's manager at Crabtree Wharf (a strategically placed docking point for trading vessels on the banks of the Thames) and a future Chelsea director, appearing on the leases.

In February 1904, at the annual meeting of the London Athletic Club, the club committee proclaimed that the club was seeking new accommodation within a few miles of Stamford Bridge. It also announced that their former ground would be handed over to Mears ('the builder') on 24 June that year. The deeds were drawn up in the name of Henry Augustus Mears, with Mears providing assurances that the LAC would be able to continue using the stadium.

The first thing Mears did was sell a huge

quantity of sand from the Stamford Bridge site to the building trade. This had been lying just a foot underground and went down as far as the water table. Some saw this activity as demonstrating that the site was being cleared for house building and accused Mears of making huge amounts of money out of this trade. But in fact the whole of the sports and football ground had been left untouched in terms of sand carting. Mears ended up covering thousands of pounds' worth of sand as he focused on building up the stadium's banking. Not one load was lifted from the stadium area itself. It seemed the legend of the 'great sand exploitation' was derived from the huge sand-pit Mears owned just off Seagrave Road that backed on to the Stamford Bridge.

It appears that the Mears family were not totally sure what they might do with the site and kept their options open. However, although it had taken years, a vision was budding into reality and a definite start had been made. From this point, the pace at which a professional football team came into being and grew to be seen as a vibrant and exciting entity was astounding.

2
BLUE DAWN

Unlike other clubs, Chelsea came from nowhere.

Len Goulden (Chelsea, 1945–50)

The very first foundations of Chelsea Football Club were laid at a Sunday-morning meeting at Stamford Bridge in 1905, which took place on newly purchased land between the man who then owned the plot, entrepreneur Gus Mears, and Frederick W. Parker, a noted financier and the official steward at the London Athletic Club (said to be one of the 'most popular starters' with the LAC) that had been situated at the Bridge before Mears acquired the property. It seemed Mears had received a lucrative offer from the Great Western

Railway Company for the whole site to be developed as a coal and goods siding and, despite his enthusiasm that was shared by his older brother JT to own a sports stadium, as he could find no one willing to help him develop the site, he had decided to sell.

A quick sale to the Great Western Railway would have realised a swift and relatively handsome profit and Mears certainly went into it in great detail, as evidenced by his proposal to remove all the sand from the site, a valuable commodity at that time, before selling to the railway.

Parker was to recollect what he saw as his last attempt to save his dream: 'I met him [Gus] by appointment one Sunday morning when we had the whole of the old grounds and adjoining vast market gardens, also purchased by him, to ourselves. He told me no one else would "come in with him", so he would accept the GW Railway offer for the whole site as a coal and goods siding, after removing the sand which extended from a foot underground right down to water.'

After listening to Fred wax lyrical about the future and the possibilities of renting out the stadium after redevelopment, Gus told his friend that he thought Parker's projection that they could take receipts of 'at least £3,000' for Cup Finals and maybe good income for international matches was 'fallacious' and it seemed that he had already made up his mind about the future of the site. However, Parker's influence would have an unexpected impact that day, although not by way of any detailed financial arguments or persuasion about the potential income that could be generated through a new stadium; Gus's opinion was to be swayed by the consequence of a totally random, if slightly inexplicable event.

As the two men were walking away from Stamford Bridge, Parker was attacked and bitten in the leg by Bluey, Mears's Aberdeen terrier. Parker later looked back on the incident: 'Feeling sad that the old ground would soon be no more, I walked slowly by his [Mears's] side when his dog, coming up from behind unobserved, bit me so severely through my cycling stockings as to draw blood freely.'

Parker informed his pal, 'Your damned dog has bitten me, look!' And he showed him the blood.

As Fred assessed his bloody injuries, alongside the disappointment of seeing his great vision being eaten up by the railways, Gus 'instead of expressing concern ... casually observed' as if the attack was to be expected, 'Scotch terrier ... always bites before he speaks.'

Parker remembered, 'The utter absurdity of the remark struck me as so genuinely funny that, although hopping about on one foot and feeling the blood trickling down, I had to laugh heartily and tell him he was the "coolest fish" I'd ever met. A minute later, he amazed me by slapping me on the shoulder and saying, "You took that damned well, Fred; most men would have kicked up hell about it. Look here, I'll stand on your judgement about Stamford Bridge. Go to the chemist and get that bite seen to and meet me here tomorrow morning at nine. Then we'll get busy."'

Certainly, up to then, it seems that Mears had no thoughts of forming a new football club by the name of Chelsea or any other epithet. The district of Chelsea was still not much more than a village and all England's major football games were played at Crystal Palace at this time.

Gus Mears's obituary in the *Fulham Chronicle* told a slightly different story of events: 'How and when the idea of starting a football club first suggested itself to him is not definitely known. But it was generally agreed that the directors of Fulham FC first mooted the idea of football at Stamford Bridge. They were at the time desirous of leaving Craven Cottage and approached Mr Mears with a view to securing a lease on his newly acquired land. Mr Mears considered the suggestion, but came to the conclusion that he would do better to start a football club himself.'

It is likely that both versions of how Stamford Bridge came to be built have elements of truth and that they are entwined in their detail. However, in 1904, Mears had openly promised to spend as much as £100,000 (a phenomenal amount of money at that time) to make Stamford Bridge a stadium that could be compared to any in the world. It seemed Gus might have had it in mind to develop a national stadium that could house any number of events and that would provide not only entertainment, but also a massive boost for the local economy and general development of the area (in which his family had a hefty stake) and an income from leasing or renting the stadium. This makes logical sense as the then current national stadium, Crystal Palace, was provoking growing discontent. It was able to accommodate crowds of up to 115,000, but it was badly designed and poorly located in terms of transport.

Nevertheless, it seems that, at the same time as the construction of the new stadium was taking place, discussions with John Dean and other directors of Fulham FAC were initiated. JT Mears's company had laid out Craven Cottage in 1896 and the new plan was to transplant the Southern League club from their ancestral home on a lease agreement to Stamford Bridge at an annual rent of £1,500 for 'their club matches only' with Gus Mears retaining the right to stage 'extraneous matches' in the stadium (this would probably include Cup Finals and international games for instance). Dean was certain that Mears would accept a lower rent, and he was possibly correct, but according to Parker he advised his friend not to compromise: 'You have the finest ground in the kingdom. If they won't come to terms, then tell them we'll start a new club that is bound to become one of the best in the country.'

But negotiations with Fulham broke down when the Fulham chairman HG Norris considered the money Mears was asking for to be too much for the Cottagers (the breaking point appears to have been Mears's insistence on keeping the revenue from other lettings).

Norris was a well-known, if not notorious figure in London football. He was a rich South London property developer who was with the Cottagers during their consecutive Southern League title victories of 1905/06 and 1906/07, and the club's subsequent election to the Football League. He then attempted to merge Fulham with Arsenal but when this didn't happen he joined the Arsenal board and went on to become chairman of the Gunners. He was behind the club's move from Woolwich to Highbury and for a short while he ran both Fulham and Arsenal before pressure forced his resignation from the Fulham board. Norris was the Mayor of Fulham from 1909 and a member of the Conservative & Unionist party. He went on to become MP for East Fulham in 1918. When the professional game recommenced after the War in 1919, he negotiated Arsenal a place in the First Division regardless of the fact that Tottenham had a much stronger case for inclusion among the elite, having won the Southern League Division One in 1900, the FA Cup in 1901, the

Western League in 1904 and having produced around a dozen international players since 1882; the Gunners' record was nowhere near this quality. ('Lucky Arsenal'?)

Norris's career in football ended in 1927 when he was banned from the game after financial irregularities at Highbury came to light.

At the time of the negotiations, Norris's decision was odd, given the position Fulham Football Club found itself in. They were not going to cash in on major games at Craven Cottage, just as they wouldn't at Stamford Bridge, which, as such, would not have been a loss, and the Fulham ground was in need of a deal of attention as a structure. On Wednesday, 4 January 1905, the Fulham Football and Athletic Club had appeared before the West London Police Court, charged by the London County Council in respect of the state of the grandstand at Craven Cottage, 'it being contended that there was no licence authorising the retention of the stand and an order was sought for its demolition'. The stand's structure amounted to four small wooden stands, bolted together under an iron roof!

The case was adjourned for three weeks in which

time Fulham contracted Archibald Leitch (the same man who would design the East Stand at Stamford Bridge) who declared the Craven Cottage stand unsafe. Fulham were given six months to tear down their decrepit apology for a stand.

Clearly, Norris had another agenda and Mears was both frustrated and disappointed at the outcome of his negotiations with Fulham. At the same time he had not been able to attract money from the City for the redevelopment project in which he had already invested heavily. As such he had to question the viability of his ideas. He decided to sell out and give Parker and his brother JT first option, before accepting the railway company's offer. Fred was still keen to stick with the idea of constructing a stadium, but later recalled that just as he couldn't convince Gus of the proposal he was also unable to sell JT the vision of 'the almost certain prospects of making immense profits on the deal'. Parker had decided to make his last shot at persuading his friend at the Sunday-morning meeting at Stamford Bridge and it was at this crucial moment that Bluey had done his stuff.

With Gus Mears supplying the finance and

Parker the energetic enthusiasm, the seeds of Chelsea Football Club were sown.

Mears determined to form a new football club, but unsurprisingly their footballing neighbours were not happy at the prospect. Fulham officials warned that they would prevent the projected new club from being admitted to any league. 'Simple Simon's Peep-Show' in the *Fulham Chronicle* echoed the sentiments of the time:

It must be amusing to cynical people to listen to the mutual recriminations between the supporters of the Fulham Football Club and the promoters of the future Kensington Football Club [the latter was one of the prospective names for Mears's proposed club]. Mr Mears, who owns the old London Athletic Club ground at Stamford Bridge, proposes to run the new club – or the new club proposes to run Mr Mears, I am not quite sure which – in rivalry with the Fulham Football and Athletic Company Limited, a flourishing business concern which naturally objects.

I should think it probable that the Granville music-hall proprietors also objected when a rival party of financiers proposed to build the Chelsea Palace. However, the Chelsea Palace was built, and the probability is that in the long run the competition will do business good.

Some sportsmen appear to find a cause of offence in the fact that a club called 'Kensington' will finance a ground in Fulham. For my part I cannot see why a club called 'Kensington' should not finance a ground in Zululand and play a team of Fiji Islanders. What's in a name when you are dealing with football? Isn't football sport, and isn't sport the same noble exciting glorious pastime whatever title you choose?

As a person with rabid opinions about football I am delighted with the scheme, for I perceive magnificent possibilities. When eleven burly ruffians from anywhere but Fulham meet eleven burly ruffians from anywhere but Kensington may I be there to see!

I should prefer Walham Green Broadway for the venue. It would provide plenty of room, and I might get a friend to give me a seat out of harm's way in one of the windows. I love sport of the right kind.

3
BREAKFAST WITH ARCHIE

Chelsea's Chelsea, ain't it.

Micky Droy (Chelsea, 1970–85)

In February 1905, collaborating with Parker and his brother JT, over a porridge and haddock breakfast in a Glasgow hotel, Gus Mears recruited the Scottish architect who had designed dozens of football stadia, including the three biggest football arenas in the world, Hampden Park, Ibrox and Celtic Park, Archibald Leitch, the legendary 'Engineering Archie', to design a new East Stand as the centrepiece of Stamford Bridge among its three enormous open terraces.

The construction stuck very much to the Leitch

formula, including his trademark pedimented centre gable on the roof. The new stand would be 120 yards long (the length of the touchline along the eastern side of the ground) and accommodate 5,000 spectators. Its roof would be suspended on great iron columns 70 feet from the ground. There were also plans to cover the opposite side of the ground at a later date to shield 50,000 fans from the weather. But on the west side of the ground crowds would remain exposed to the elements for many years to come.

The Bridge, with a proposed capacity of 95,000, was to be England's second largest venue after Crystal Palace. It was built, like its Glaswegian cousins, in a bowl shape. The construction, with its distinctive East Stand, would be a constant reminder of the massive gamble the Mears family had undertaken. The dressing rooms were placed so that the teams always emerged from the stand. The pitch was laid by 'Scotch workmen' with 'special turf' that had been brought, 'regardless of cost, from Winchester'.

Gus Mears wanted his stadium to have an awe-inspiring effect 'that would stagger humanity'. This was development on a grand scale, a construction that would become the pride of London and one of the seminal sites in terms of the history of the game.

Almost unlimited material for the building of the enormous terracing of the three exposed sides of the stadium became available from the clay excavated from the new Piccadilly Underground railway line. Mears didn't pay for any of the material used for the foundations of the Bridge; in fact, he was even being paid to cart it away. To move the material from the tube excavations was earning him at least one shilling per load but this saved the excavators a trip of several miles to deposit the rubble. Transporting and dumping was a major expense in the construction of the tube and Mears probably did very well out of the situation. JT Mears had also contracted (and so was paid) for the removal of the clay from the Kingsway tunnel then being constructed, transporting it in his own lorries to a pier close to the Temple station, from where it was carried upriver by barge to his Crabtree Wharf at Fulham, and from there removed to Stamford Bridge. Cinders were transported from a local sewer and rubble from other building sites was also used, including that from the Georgian mansion of Lord Phillimore, which was being demolished by Mears.

During that demolition, a workman stuck a pick into the plaster of a wall which threw forth a shower of hundreds of spade (or 'Spade Ace') guineas that were issued at the latter end of the 1700s. The coins were in close to mint condition. They were immediately mistakenly believed to be 'Hanover jacks', brass discs used as counters in upper-class card games. The workmen filled their pockets with these and passed them on to their children as playthings. One site worker was said to have carried some away in a horse's nosebag while others punched holes in them to decorate the harnesses of their horses. A good number of the guineas were likely to have ended up buried around 30 feet under the Stamford Bridge site probably beneath the West Stand. If anyone digs them up in the future, they will certainly be worth a few bob.

Without a doubt, the greatest asset of the new stadium was its location. Chelsea's first handbook declared that 'All roads lead to Stamford Bridge' and provided details of the railway connections to Chelsea and Fulham station (opposite the main entrance) and Walham Green (now Fulham Broadway). It also told how omnibuses pass 'the Grounds every few minutes of the day from all parts of London' and 'River Thames Steamboats call at Chelsea Pier' (the steamboats were owned by none other than JT Mears, who was also a Chelsea director).

The ample transport links put Stamford Bridge within relatively easy reach of the whole of the western half of London, and offered uncomplicated access for much of the rest of the capital. As such, Chelsea has habitually drawn its support from right across London, only being stopped by very traditional hotbeds of support for clubs deeply ingrained in the local community (such as the East End and Islington). But, in the first decade of Blue history, the population living close to and around Stamford Bridge were those most likely to stand on the great terraces on a regular basis.

In March 1905, Mears backed up his assurances that the London Athletic Club would be able to maintain its association with the Bridge by signing an agreement that guaranteed that the LAC could continue to operate at the stadium for the next seven years and demonstrated his good faith by laying a new cinder running track for the commencement of the 1905 summer season.

Mears would make big money from renting his stadium and his aim was to manage the biggest and best stadium in London and perhaps the world. But he was also committed to sport and, while this is unlikely to have transcended his commercial ambitions, profit was not his only motive. He invested a fortune of his own money in the Bridge, but his creation gave him status as well as adding to his profile enormously and he enjoyed that. During most events at the stadium, he could invariably be seen, his straw hat on his head, walking round the premises, his huge cigar in hand, passing the time with people.

4
THE BIRTH OF
THE BLUES

It's no good playing well one week and rubbish
the next. We need the consistency or you will get fans
saying that they should have been here the week
before and not coming back.

John Hollins (Chelsea, 1963–75 & 1983–84)

On 14 March 1905 at 7.30 p.m., the first
meeting of the new club took place at The
Rising Sun pub (now The Butcher's Hook),
opposite the present-day main entrance to
Stamford Bridge on Fulham Road; this was the
birth of the Blues.

William Claude Kirby (who, like Fred Parker, had

been an official at the London Athletic Club) was appointed chairman, a position he would hold until his death in 1935, while Gus Mears was named a director and overall patron (he would maintain general control of the club until his death in 1912); Parker took the post of honorary financial secretary and Lord Cadogan was named as President. In 1900, Cadogan had become the first Mayor of Chelsea; his descendant the Eighth Earl derives much of his personal fortune, close to £1.4 billion (making him one of the wealthiest individuals in Britain), from the land Cadogan owned in the Chelsea area. His Lordship's light-blue racing colours were chosen for the new club's shirts (the side wore white shorts in the first years of its history) but this was changed to royal blue in 1912 (at which point Chelsea took on the title of 'the Blues' in popular parlance). However, it is also possible that the incentive for adopting blue as the club colour was in honour of Bluey, the little Scots terrier whose seeming dislike for the Great Western Railway (and/or his latent love of football), which gave rise to sudden, unexpected belligerence, had indirectly started it all.

Starting a professional football club at that time

was a bold move, especially considering that Mears could have made a quick profit selling to the railways. The professional game had only been established in 1884 after rebel clubs had mutinied against the Football Association which had ruled that players should only be paid their expenses and in the South East the game was still chiefly an amateur pursuit.

The club was floated on a share issue of 5,000 £1 shares and a guess at the interest in the sale can be drawn from the fact that half of the capital was subscribed at the first meeting.

The Chelsea Pensioner was chosen as the club's crest and this gave rise to the side's original nickname. The crest was never to appear on the players' kit, but it would remain in use for the next half-century, since which time the official club badge has changed three times.

Naming the new club had been one of the first vital tasks. Fulham was, of course, already in existence and a close neighbour, so early suggestions of Fulham Road Rangers and the curious Fulham Strollers were non-starters. London FC (a title Arsenal considered in the 1930s) and West London Wanderers were thought to be presumptuous. Kensington and Stamford Bridge FC was another consideration, but the shout of 'Play up Kensington and Stamford Bridge' hardly tripped off the tongue. Just calling the club Stamford Bridge felt like the path of least resistance, and was the most popular title among the organising committee, there being a feeling that it was a name known all round the world and one that would attract attention to the stadium. But Parker was concerned about the possibility that connections would be made with the village of the same name in Yorkshire, and he argued that most of the post addressed to him at Stamford Bridge had been subject to delay and needed written instructions to redirect it. This was generally written 'not Stamford Bridge, Yorks; try Stamford Bridge Grounds, Walham Green, London'.

Interestingly enough, Walham Green was never considered; Kensington FC was mooted and, although that was the name that appeared to be most popular with the public, it seemingly didn't find favour among the committee.

Some have argued that the club secretary William Lewis, who had come from Brentford to assist the SW6 club in canvassing the Southern

League for entry to its ranks, suggested the name Chelsea FC. His appointment was a bit of a surprise. In service of the Bees, he had been chairman, secretary, manager and director at different times and there had been problems when Lewis had requested 'consent in writing to continue his engagement with Lord and Messrs A & L Rothschild' (Lord Rothschild was the patron of the Griffin Park club). The Chelsea board had requested their solicitors 'to ascertain from Mr Lewis the nature of this engagement, and how much time, in his opinion, it was likely to absorb'.

Others have claimed it was Parker who came up with the idea of naming the club Chelsea, but this was met with a chorus of 'No, no!' Another story has it that Fred put forward Chelsea Athletic (understandable given his affinity with and hopes for athletics at the Bridge), while Mears came up with Chelsea Rovers and the matter was settled by Lewis's suggestion to drop the appendages, and so Chelsea it was.

It was written at the time, 'So Mr H A Mears's football club is to be called Chelsea FC, although it will be no more connected with the adjoining borough than with Timbuktu.'

On 11 March 1905, *The Times* declared, 'It has been decided to form a professional football club, called the Chelsea Football Club, for Stamford-bridge. Application will be made for admission to the first division of the Southern League.'

On 7 April, the *West London & Fulham Times* reflected, 'A great deal has been written and much more said as to the chances of the Chelsea FC for admission to the Southern League, but the recent appointment of Mr William Lewis, of Brentford, to the secretaryship of the club, has aroused the keenest interest ... It is common knowledge that "Jock" Robertson, the well-known Scotch International, was the successful candidate for Managerial honours.'

Although John ('Jock'/'Jackie') Tait Robertson was named as Chelsea's player/secretary-manager on 27 March, he would not be confirmed in his position at Stamford Bridge until League status had been confirmed.

Working with due haste, on 19 April 1905, four Manchester and Liverpool clubs were canvassed by Parker and Robertson in an effort to elicit a favourable response for the club's application to join the Football League, although negotiations had also started for entry to the Southern League; this was a time of 'belt and braces' diplomacy. The following day, they went to Lytham, Preston and Blackburn. Robertson had to play for his then employers Glasgow Rangers that evening, so Parker dealt with Blackpool, Bolton, Derby, Small Heath and West Bromwich Albion single-handedly.

At the same time, Robertson started to sign players, and pulled together a strong nucleus of experienced professionals. For a wage of £4 per week, Robertson came to West London from North of the Border in the spring of 1905. Some have claimed that it was never the plan for him to remain at Stamford Bridge for an extended period, but this may have been a cover story to divert from his eventual unexpected departure. However, his long and illustrious playing career had provided him with good connections in the game and, working alongside trainer Harry Ransom, he provided Chelsea with the staff profile for a Football League set-up.

But the Football League was apprehensive given Chelsea's flirtations with the Southern League. Secretary Lewis had indeed been asked to lobby the Southern League on Chelsea's behalf, but Parker had already canvassed the clubs in the Southern League and concluded that the majority were supporting Fulham who proposed that no new members should be elected from the London area. This was why he was chasing recruitment to the Football League.

By this time Chelsea had made an application to join the Southern League which had predictably met with opposition from other London clubs including Spurs and Fulham; and, of course, Fulham chairman Henry Norris's refusal to lease Stamford Bridge had in effect helped to motivate Mears to start his own club.

Part of Parker's purpose for the tour of League clubs had been to test the reaction to the possibility of Chelsea joining that particular 'band of brothers'. But in truth the approaches to join the Southern League could hardly have been expected to garner unbridled support as all the London clubs of any standing were already members of that fraternity. On the other hand, in Divisions One and Two of the Football League (the only two divisions in those days), Woolwich Arsenal were the only representative of the capital city (although Leyton Orient would be admitted at the start of the 1905/06 season). The only other League club south of Birmingham was Bristol City, and the Football League was keen to expand its influence into the South East.

It was during their canvassing that Parker and Robertson met Lytham's JJ Bentley, the president of the Football League, who asked insistently, 'Your new club is trying to run with the hare and hunt with the hounds. Which are you really going for, the Southern League or us?'

Bentley's question prompted Parker to show a commitment to the Football League and he immediately returned to his hotel and telephoned the London Press Agency to announce that Chelsea would not be pursuing election to the Southern League but instead would look for entry to the 'Football League only'.

5
FOOTBALL LEAGUE VIA 'SCOTCH-AND-POLLIES'

I think Chelsea players play lovely football but sometimes you do not get much joy from watching their game because the other team is not playing how they normally play.

Gianfranco Zola (Chelsea, 1996–2003)

There were some notable football officials who believed that Chelsea were being impudent by seeking election to the Football League while lacking any playing pedigree. It has to be said the Stamford Bridge brigade were audacious in their ambitions, but they had the means in terms of plant and finance to back up their pretensions and early in 1905 they were not going to admit publicly that they believed their chances of being elected to the League were unrealistic.

To prove that the club was serious, players were signed up straight away. On 26 April, Bob McRoberts (Chelsea's first £100 player) a centre-forward, who was later to play in the middle of the defence, and inside-forward James Robertson (£50) from Small Heath Alliance (the club that would become Birmingham City) were signed, and, a day later, the renowned dribbler Jimmy Windridge's contract was secured for £190 (also from Small Heath). Jim was a bashful, but amiable young man, unheard of in the game in 1905, but he was to play for England two seasons later and was nicknamed 'Windridge the Wizard'. A few weeks later, the left-wing pair, Davie Copeland and John 'Jack' Kirwan, from the 1901 Tottenham Cup-winning side, were also recruited alongside Scottish defenders Bob Mackie, Tommy Miller and George Key.

At the board meeting on Wednesday, 17 May 1905, the secretary-manager announced he had added the following players to his squad: Micky

Byrne, Tommy Miller, Jimmy Watson, Jim Craigie, Frank Woolf, Charlie Donaghy (recorded as Donoghue in the minute book), David Copeland, John Kirwan (spelled Kirwin in the minute book; he would be the first Chelsea player to be selected to play for Ireland – he was to win four caps in all, the first against England in 1906) and Bob McEwan. It was also recorded that 'The Manager reported that he had canvassed the Clubs in the 1st and 2nd Division of the League and that he had received the promise of support from a large number of clubs.'

Under the heading 'Canvass Clubs', it was minuted: 'Resolved that The Manager be instructed to continue canvassing Clubs in the League and to use his utmost endeavours to obtain their support at the forthcoming Meeting of the Football Association.'

The word 'Association' was crossed out and 'League' inserted above, then initialled by the chairman William Kirby. This was a clear sign that all the Pensioners' eggs had been placed in the basket labelled 'Football League'.

It was at this meeting that the signing of William Foulke was announced. He was probably the most notable West London import of the club's early years.

Sheffield United's Willie 'Fatty' Foulke was a gigantic goalkeeper whose name would be associated with Stamford Bridge forever. An English international, who before coming to London had appeared in three Cup Finals (he had two winners medals) with Sheffield United, including the 1901 defeat against Tottenham (after a replay), Willie gained national fame for his enormous stature and strength (in those days men of such 'Dreadnought' qualities were uncommon). Standing more than 6ft 2in and weighing in at over 22 stone, he was a colossus of the game and a legend in his own knickers (as football shorts were then referred to). It is unlikely that Chelsea have made a better pound-for-pound buy at fifty quid. It was reported that when Fred Parker first met his new keeper he gasped a whisper, 'My word! Darkness covers the earth!'

All Chelsea's activity and expenditure combined as a huge act of faith as election to the League was still far from a certainty (although a number of signings had been made on the condition that Chelsea gained election). It was no easy task to gain admittance to the League and the clubs who had gained entry to the privileged strata of the game didn't take kindly to ambitious 'Johnny-come-latelies' who might seek to join their exclusive (and increasingly lucrative) fellowship.

Parker recalled the crucial evening at the Tavistock Hotel, Covent Garden Plaza, London, on 29 May 1905, before the meeting that would decide his club's fate: 'Eve of League meeting was a trying one. Representatives of all clubs seeking election were "pushing the boat out" freely until well past three a.m.

'Claude Kirby came to me in the small hours very perturbed because several of the wagging tongues – belonging in some cases to clubs who had promised us a vote – were saying to one another: "Chelsea? Let 'em wait a year or two. Cheek, trying to get into the League before kicking a ball."

'I told him not to worry for I had heard them and noticed they were the Managers of clubs, not those who would have the votes.'

Following this determined, last-minute canvassing (where Parker ensured delegates were plied with more than adequate libation to oil the wheels of his club's acceptance during those intense after-hours lobbying), a prolonged Football League Annual General Meeting, made up of mostly men from the Northern and Midlands heartlands of the game, was addressed by Frederick Parker, who, along with Claude Kirby, was representing Chelsea's bid. Parker had to prepare his words on the shortest of notice from his chairman (just prior to the critical meeting) who having made his excuses had designated Fred for the job he should probably have done himself. However, Parker's telling of his approach to the meeting suggested that he was unfazed by the gravity of the situation: 'Claude sprang it on me he had to go to the office, so I should have to make the speech. Didn't worry me a bit, and I walked in whistling and humming "the clans they are gatherin'".

However, Fred's months of preparation must have provided him with the confidence that comes with the laying of a secure grounding. In competition with a host of other clubs looking to be admitted into the Football League, Parker's arguments were straightforward and clear, emphasising three vital elements of his club's claims for elevation. In his words, 'I simply told them the three points they [the clubs] would naturally wish to be satisfied on.'

First, he talked of Chelsea's financial stability, informing those present that the club had more than £3,000 in the bank. Second, his small moustache perhaps twitching with passion, Parker told of a group visit to Stamford Bridge, 'Many of those present had accepted our invitation the previous day, Sunday, and expressed themselves that even in its unfinished state it would clearly bear comparison with any club in the League.' As such, Chelsea's ground was seen to be fit for purpose and ready to house a team to compete at the highest level.

Finally, he assured the representatives from the member clubs that Chelsea also had a team of a standard to equip themselves well against any potential opposition, taking the time to read out a list of the players thus far signed to the club's cause; according to Fred, these were 'the only notes I had prepared'. He went on, 'When Mr Bentley gently remarked "Your three minutes are up, Mr Parker", I bowed and said, "I thank you all for listening so attentively to me and will not trespass on you further, beyond suggesting –" as I started walking out "– that when you consider the points I have laid before you, you will come to the conclusion that you really cannot refuse us."'

In fact, Parker had overrun the time he had been given to make his club's case by three minutes (quite a lot considering that he had originally been allotted just three minutes in all!) but a few of his audience were as good as dozing off after the long and exhausting event (and the 'exertions' of the previous evening).

Parker later remembered that, after he had exited, 'Tommy Barcroft, who came out of the room while the counting was on, was kind enough to tell me I made the best speech of the lot, and he thought us certain to be elected.'

The thrust of Fred's strategy from the beginning had been Chelsea's role in fighting the battle of the Football League to become established in the capital. It was a strong card to hold as was the facility Stamford Bridge offered the League as a venue.

Throughout the extended proceedings, Kirby had been tearing between the Tavistock and his office by Hansom cab; both he and Jock

Robertson were not totally certain about Chelsea's chances. But most people involved with the voting felt that Leeds City and Chelsea were pretty much certainties. It was thought that either Hull City or Burslem Port Vale were destined to take the third place. The size of the populations that clubs might call on for support was a crucial factor equal only to the need for a firm financial foundation. Providing competition for rugby was a factor but very much a secondary consideration. As such, Chelsea were high scorers on the two most important criteria for League membership at that time and the voting reflected this, although things weren't as clear-cut as many had prophesied: Leeds City 26; Burslem Port Vale 21; Chelsea 20; Hull City 18; Stockport County 13; Doncaster Rovers (who were seeking re-election) 4; Clapton Orient 1.

Chelsea were in, but Parker's oratory and commitment looked to have been critical. To the chagrin of some, the Pensioners became full accredited members of the Football League, having only been in existence for two months. Years after, Parker, writing to a friend, confessed, 'I took the precaution to bribe the girl behind the bar that night, so that whenever I called for so many "Scotch-and-pollies" the glass on the extreme left should always be a Ross's Dry Ginger. So I was able to keep my head clear.'

As such, Fred was likely to have been one of the few men in the room both fully awake and free of the effects of alcohol, which after a long day would have left people more in the mood for a lie-down than a protracted debate. He was a self-assured man and he demonstrated this by laying wagers with Kirby and Jock Robertson, in the presence of hot competition, that Chelsea would realise their ambition. Fred recalled, 'Going down to K's bedroom before breakfast I found him and Robertson looking like men waiting the hangmen, both saying we'd not be elected. I laughed at them and said: "Bet you five bob each we do".'

After the vote, a proposal from Mr CE Sutcliffe, the Division Two representative on the Management Committee, supporting an increase in the number of clubs in the Division from 36 to 40 was discussed. Thirty-one votes out of 37 were cast in favour. As such Leeds City, Hull City, Clapton Orient and Stockport County were elected to the League. This was a hugely progressive move for the Football League. Over several years, there had been pressure to increase the number of clubs taking part in the League in order that promotion and relegation might be introduced without the chance of any covert manipulation between clubs. So, in effect, Parker's role, at least at the Tavistock Hotel that evening in securing Chelsea's admission, had been more symbolic than decisive.

But Parker's efforts went back to his run-in with Bluey and they gave rise to what was quite a special first victory. It had taken just two months for the club to be accepted into the League, and, although Fred's financial backing and drive should not be underestimated, it was Gus Mears, even though he had initially had no plans to create a football club, who was to be the official founder and sole proprietor of Chelsea Football Club. Three decades later, Parker wrote, 'Mr Mears was truly the Father of the Club but I can claim to be its Godfather.' As is well known among football aficionados, the Mears name was to have a long association with Chelsea up to his great-grandson Brian Mears who finally left the club after a boardroom coup in 1981.

A sporting but also expedient footnote to the

event at the Tavistock was Fred Parker's offer
(together with the representative from Clapton
Orient – both London clubs feeling the
responsibility of hosts to the meeting) to pay the
travelling expenses of Chelsea's opponents for
election to the Second Division. Chelsea and
Clapton Orient's election was something of a coup
in a competition dominated by Northern and
Midland clubs, but that didn't mean all of them
were happy about it.

During the celebrations that followed, Mears
made a sobering statement to the jubilant
gathering; looking out at the new Stamford Bridge
nearing completion, he said, 'Well, that's that.
Now for the struggle. I suppose the first five years
will be the worst.'

It was now also time to think about getting
some income. Ground season tickets were sold at
half a guinea for men, 10s 6d for ladies and
schoolboys for the grandstand, and 10s 6d and 5s
6d for the ground only.

At the inaugural Chelsea board meeting as a
Football League club on Thursday, 1 June 1905, it
was minuted under 'Payment of Clubs': 'It was
resolved that £20 be paid to Northern and £15 to

Midland Clubs respectively on their visiting the Club grounds to play League matches, for three years commencing on 1st September 1905.'

That day the club's bank balance was £1,419-11s-8d in credit. The company seal was officed to the Counterpart Lease of Stamford Bridge between Mr HA Mears and the Company. The rent to Chelsea FC was £2,000 per year.

In a preview of the 1905/06 season, the *Athletic News* (the pre-eminent journal in terms of football at the time) announced: 'Never in the history of the game has a club been started under more favourable surroundings. Thanks to the enterprise of Mr H A Mears the club will have one of the best equipped grounds in the country. Mr Mears evidently does not believe in doing things by halves and has spared no expense in the furtherance of his hobby.

'The ground when finished will be one of the most capacious in the country. Outside the running path, which by the way is a quarter of a mile round, there will be no fewer than 60 tiers of terracing for two-thirds of the circumference, while the covered stand will hold no fewer than 5,000 spectators.

'The dressing rooms are replete with every convenience including plunge as well as hot and cold baths.'

On 2 August, it was reported that the pitch had already been marked out and that 'the famous green-sward is just now looking delightfully green and fresh'.

The next day the initial statutory meeting for shareholders was convened at Stamford Bridge. Claude Kirby, as the club chairman, showed the happy band around the newly refurbished stadium which was then close to completion. The press were informed that everyone was delighted with the facilities for the public and the players and the quality of the construction work.

But secretly the directors were worried as there had been a series of delays and problems with the construction of the stand and it was a close-run thing whether the ground would be ready for use by the September start to the season. However, by 30 August, when the press were invited by the club 'to view the grounds', the Bridge was prepared for its first League campaign.

The playing staff had started training on 5 August and were reported to be 'raring to go'.

Robertson had asked local players to take part in two exclusive trial matches which attracted a good number of hopefuls.

Looking forward to the season, Robertson wrote, 'It may be said that nothing is certain in football, and therefore no one can be sure of success; but, at any rate, Chelsea are determined to deserve it.'

6
FIRST FOUGHT, STOCKPORT

Chelsea get beaten by goals that should have never been given or at least one they should have scored.

Ian Portafield (Chelsea manager, 1991–93)

1905/06

Chelsea's first competitive match, on 2 September 1905, was not the memorable occasion it perhaps should have been. In those days, players and manager were often obliged to walk from the railway station to the ground for away matches, not unusually through the dingy industrial districts of working-class towns like Stockport. Willie Foulke, the Pensioners' massive keeper, was stalking forebodingly through the Cheshire town, when a young Hatters supporter shouted, 'Eee, you'll get licked t'day!'

Foulke was quick to reply, 'Then it will be for the first time for Chelsea, m'lad.'

The line-up for the match was:

STOCKPORT COUNTY: Albert Pemble; James Haywood, Waters, Stuart, Thomas Hall, Ernest (Eddie) Cresser, Schofield, Fred Crump, Robert Manson, George Dodd, Edwin Bardsley

CHELSEA: William Foulke; Robert Mackie, Marshall McEwan, George Key, Robert McRoberts, Thomas Miller, Martin Moran, John Tait Robertson, James Copeland, James Windridge, John Kirwan

The 7,000 attendance at Edgeley Park was a record for the ground, evidence of the huge interest in the Blue newcomers to the Football League. A lot of publicity had accompanied Chelsea into the 'big-time', but as it turned out the Londoners, under the captainship of Foulke, were unable to live up to their promotional hype.

From the moment the referee, Mr D Hammond of

Heywood, started the game, the visitors looked anxious, playing in what felt like an overcautious way. The lively Stockport attack took full advantage of the Pensioners' immobile defence, but this gave the Northern spectators the opportunity to watch the gargantuan Chelsea custodian do his stuff, and Willie did well to deal with a number of dangerous shots, particularly one low powerful drive that he had to work hard to stop.

The first half was goalless, although Cresser, Stockport's energetic wing-half, had scraped the bar. However, the home side swiftly took the lead following the break after Schofield was blatantly clattered in the penalty box. The County winger got up to take the spot-kick himself, which was duly saved by Foulke, but Bardsley's cross from the rebound found George Dodd and the man who would later wear the blue of Chelsea easily put his side in front.

The Pensioners started to put some moves together towards the end of the match, particularly down the right side, where veteran Dave Copeland and Martin Moran combined well, and with a clear chance it was only Moran's poor finishing that robbed the visitors of an equaliser.

Although there was some agreement that it had been 'a terribly hard game' for Chelsea and individually some of the London side had looked promising, it was clear that, as a team, the lads from SW6 had a lot of work to do.

Although they lost their initial competitive game, Chelsea would go half-a-dozen League matches without tasting a second defeat.

On Monday, 4 September, Chelsea's founder, Gus Mears, kicked off the first game Chelsea played at Stamford Bridge, a friendly against Liverpool. The Reds, who had been beaten 3–1 at Woolwich Arsenal the previous Saturday, were the Second Division Champions of 1904/05 and the team that would be League Champions at the end of the 1905/06 term, the first team to achieve this feat (and it wasn't repeated until Everton won the League in 1932). Liverpool were beaten 4–0 at the Bridge; the match receipts amounted to £102 and (very oddly to the modern perception) JJ Bentley, the Football League President, ran the line. The first Chelsea goal to be scored at Stamford Bridge (a Liverpool strike having been disallowed) was claimed by the Pensioners' centre-half Bob McRoberts, and he was to get another before the game was over. Windridge and Moran completed the decisive victory.

Liverpool had agreed to take half the gate receipts with a minimum retainer of £50, and they returned North with a cheque for £51-3s-9d.

In the same month as the thrashing of the Scousers, the Bridge reverted to its former sporting role and 30-year-old George Edward Larner, who would be a double Olympic Champion in 1908, broke four world records in the walking event; the five-, six- and eight-mile distances together with the distance record covered in an hour.

The first competitive game to be contested at Stamford Bridge took place nine days after the encounter with Liverpool. This was staged after a 1-0 win over Blackpool at Bloomfield Road. Player/secretary-manager Jock Robertson scored what was Chelsea's first League goal in their first League win. Hull City were the first visitors to the home of the Pensioners. Willie Foulke was again in goal for Chelsea, giving the West London fans their first sight of the big man trundling threateningly up and down his goal-line – but it was the talented James Edwin Windridge who gave the Fulham Road supporters cause to celebrate, banging home the new club's first hat-trick in the 5–1 defeat of the Tigers, showing some extraordinary skill and poise in the process. David Campbell Copeland scored twice in front of a good crowd for a Monday afternoon (6,000).

On the evening after that match, there was a board meeting at the ground. For its 90-minute duration, the participants barely mentioned football, with the exception of deciding 'to invite the reporter of the *Fulham Chronicle* to accompany the team to Bradford'. The focus was on finances and in particular concern about the wage bill that was at the heady heights of £75-10s a week. The club had just £162-13s-1d in the bank. The fact that the Fulham Borough Band hadn't turned up the previous Saturday also provoked lengthy discussion and the secretary was told to let that particular ensemble know that their services would no longer be required at the Bridge. He was also instructed 'to communicate with other bands'.

Of course, the board had no way of knowing that the team would have the immediate popularity that was to come. On 23 September,

20,000 supporters came to watch West Bromwich Albion at the Bridge, a big Second Division crowd at that time. A 1–0 win for the home side was cause for celebration but the bank balance being boosted to almost £374 was almost better news.

Football Chat, formerly *Athletic and Sporting Chat*, a sort of early football journal, was reproduced in the programme for that game; it read, 'It would be interesting to know if Chelsea's popularity is brought about by newspapers booming, Foulke's name, or curiosity to see the team who are being provided with the most palatial home of any club playing football.'

In keeping with the stadium's history of sporting diversity, during October, Middlesex played the 'Original' New Zealand All Blacks at the new Stamford Bridge. The Kiwis won 34–0. In fact, the tourists only lost once, when Wales beat them 3–0, in a 32-game, four-month tour of Britain, conceding just 39 points, while scoring 830. On New Year's Day, the New Zealanders defeated France 38–8 in Paris – nothing new there then!

During November, the directors withdrew the manager's control of team affairs. At a board meeting on the 21st of that month it was recorded:

'Teams will be selected by the Directors with the assistance of the Manager.'

At that point, Robertson was fully involved as a player in addition to his secretary-manager duties and, although it was not unusual at the time for a club's board to have a say in team selection, this was a clear change in Chelsea's policy that didn't seem to have much to do with the team's performance.

TEAM-MAKER JOCK

Born in Dumbarton on 25 January 1877, John Tait ('Jackie'/'Jock') Robertson started his footballing life with Poinfield FC, Sinclair Swifts and joined Greenock Morton in 1894. Able to play at inside or outside left or left-half, between April 1898 and March 1905, Robertson won 16 Scottish caps (including an 11–0 victory over Northern Ireland in 1901) captaining his country three times and scoring on three occasions. He had also represented the Scottish League half-a-dozen times and played in the Glasgow vs. Sheffield Wednesday Inter-city Challenge twice. For Chelsea he would continue playing at left half-back, something between a left midfielder and a full-back in the contemporary game. He was known to have a fine good eye for talent and considerable contacts in the game. These were the prime reasons that the Chelsea directors brought him to London. Looking back on the building of the first Chelsea squad, he was to reflect, 'We then set to work at once on the engrossing and intensely difficult task of marshalling a strong side. In football, as in war, the crux of the matter is the men. So far, the players we have engaged have more than fulfilled expectations.'

But there were some times when serious business gave way to humorous moments. Close to Christmas 1905, Jock wrote, 'My work has not been without its amusing side.' His role included looking at some unlikely applications, often from people who were completely unsuitable. He recalled, 'Among the many applications I received was one from a man who said he was a splendid centre-forward, but if that position was not vacant he could manipulate a turnstile.'

One ambitious candidate, Jack 'Swiper' Budge, who stood a proud 3ft 2in in his stockinged feet, impressed Robertson with his ball skills but was asked to leave the Bridge following an altercation with Willie Foulke after the big man had mocked

Swiper's relative lack of physical stature; 'Thoust nought bout op to me stots' was Willie's offending remark. As the little man headed for him scowling with temper and Cockney curses, the keeper laughingly observed, 'Eee! E's gota munk on!' In the fracas that followed, the belligerent Budge inflicted a vicious bite on Foulke's left calf.

Another submission informed the Chelsea manager, 'You will be astonished to see me skip down the line like a deer.'

One keen candidate was prepared to 'be linesman, goal-keep, or mind the coats'.

An attack-minded and stylish player, Robertson had left Scotland to wear the colours of Everton, signing professional forms in October 1895. After 26 games (and one goal) for the Liverpool Blues, Jock joined Southampton for a brief spell in May 1898 and helped the Saints win the Southern League in 1899. He returned to Scotland and Rangers for a fee of £300 in August 1899 where he gained three Championship medals (1900, 1901, 1902; he also had runners-up medals for 1904 and 1905) and was part of the Gers' Scottish Cup-winning side of 1903. After half-a-dozen seasons and 130 appearances for Rangers, he made his way to the Fulham Road. Robertson did the job that was asked of him, bringing together a group of men who were mostly total strangers to each other and moulded them into an attractive and winning team that came close to promotion in their first season. While he was given ample finances to buy players, his signings nearly all justified the money paid for them.

Robertson's role was quite complex. Trainers (what would be called coaches today) had always been part of the game. They were, in the main, ex-players and, as the majority of boards had realised by 1900, these men were mostly unprepared for managing in the professional environment of the business the game had become. The 'secretary-manager' that 'innovated' out of the sport was usually a man with knowledge and experience of the game, but who could also respond to a board's wishes in terms of finding and developing players. While some boards continued to have a heavy influence on team selection, most also had other commercial interests to attend to and so needed a person who could undertake the day-to-day duties involved in running a team.

Many secretary-managers were deskbound,

dealing with transfers, publicity and low-level commercial and administrative work. They often delegated the readying of the squad to the trainers, who could usually be distinguished by their cloth-caps and roll-neck woolly jumpers. However, Robertson might be thought of as one of the first player/secretary-managers to move towards the modern idea of the manager in a tracksuit that would be associated with the management role in the contemporary game.

Chelsea competed consistently with the Second Division front-runners and attracted big crowds. The side scored 90 goals in 38 Second Division games (58 of them were netted at Stamford Bridge where Burslem Port Vale were thrashed 7–0); no club in the division had scored more. Fred Pearson was top League scorer with 18.

In that first season for Chelsea (but the 18th in the history of the Football League), the Pensioners finished third in the Second Division, nine points adrift of Manchester United, but both had been part of the fight for promotion. Bristol City had won the League, their 66 points bettering Chelsea's total by 13.

PENSIONERS PUSHING

The possibility of Chelsea winning a place in the First Division was probably what drew the fans to Stamford Bridge. The visit of the Manchester Reds, Chelsea's closest rivals for a place in the top flight (other than West Bromwich Albion who finished a point behind the Pensioners), over the Easter holidays (Good Friday, 13 April) was to produce by far the biggest gate of the season – a total of 67,000 spectators (the biggest crowd for a League game in London up to that point) – and the *Chelsea Chronicle* programme sold 11,000 copies that day. The police bill for the match amounted to £18-9s-6d, but the sorry-looking Chelsea bank account that stood at £33-15s-7d on 10 April had swollen to £1,405-14s-1d by the 20th.

However, Chelsea also pulled in the punters away from SW6. From the start of their first campaign, the Pensioners attracted great crowds all over the country. It was not unusual for their visits to Midland and Northern venues to be started with a welcome at the railway stations by huge gatherings of curious opposing fans. These were the days when anything from the 'Smoke' had an air of glamour about it and Chelsea were seen as boys from the 'big city', the 'Burlington Berts' of football and a sight to see in themselves.

The club's opening two away fixtures in the League realised record receipts for Stockport County and Blackpool and the crowds had come to the Bridge in their tens of thousands. Barnsley and Blackpool had been defeated 6–0 at the Bridge and Hull City, as detailed above, had gone down 5–1 there. The home of the Pensioners drew 25,000 fans to see the game against Bristol City (a goalless draw) and 30,000 turned up for the encounter with Glossop North End. However, Chelsea were well behind Newcastle's average of 22,000; the Magpies were a well-established First Division side (founded in 1892 from a combination of much older clubs). As such, the total of over 273,000 who attended the 19 League matches at the Bridge, an average gate of 14,368 per game (and nearly 11,000 away from home), was more than encouraging support. Supporters would travel from all over London, a relatively common practice since the London Athletic Club's sports ground had opened in 1877. And it was in the club's interest to advertise Chelsea as the best-connected side (in terms of transport) in the metropolis.

THE BIRTH OF THE BLUES

Although not in the Football League at that time, Tottenham Hotspur were probably London's leading club. In 1901, Spurs had made history as the first professional Southern team, and the first non-League club since the formation of the League, to win the FA Cup. Known as 'The Flower of the South', the North London club outshone the likes of First Division Woolwich Arsenal with their panache and association with success. But by the end of their inaugural term Chelsea could claim to be competing with Spurs in the popularity stakes. The Pensioners appeared to be an instant success and, although they were just a Second Division side, Chelsea stole the headlines wherever they went. Football programmes and local newspapers from Leyton to Manchester included the most admiring articles lauding the power of Chelsea's celebrity.

That season, the 35th FA Cup was won (for the first time) by Everton at Crystal Palace in front of 75,609 spectators. Sandy Young, who later turned out for Spurs, scored the only goal of the game in the 75th minute to send Newcastle back to the North East a disappointed side.

Chelsea had been too late with their application

for exemption from the qualifying rounds of the FA Cup that season. The Pensioners' defeated their first FA Cup opponents, the 1st Battalion Grenadiers (Moran got his team's first FA Cup goal in the 6–1 defeat of the Pongoes), and then beat Southend United to progress to the third preliminary round. Chelsea, now wanting to focus on their League commitments (the club were playing a League match against Burnley on the same day as their third preliminary-round game), fielded what was more or less a reserve side against Crystal Palace at the old Cup Final stadium. The result was to be the worst of Chelsea's opening season; Francis 'Pat' O'Hara got the consolation goal in a 7–1 defeat.

The one-sided nature of that game motivated a Football Association rule change and from then on it became an offence under FA regulations for a club to field a less than full-strength side in the FA Cup – a rule certainly not followed to the letter in recent years. This reform resulted in the dates of League and Cup fixtures being kept apart, for the early rounds at least.

However, Chelsea Football Club could not be said to have had anything less than an excellent start; they had certainly made a mark. Skilfully blending youth and experience, Jock Robertson had taken his young side close to the pinnacle of the Second Division, while also appearing regularly in the first-team.

But it seemed money worries had not been completely allayed. In the summer of 1906, Robert Bush was signed from West Ham, but he was almost immediately in dispute with the club, having not received the railway season ticket the manager had promised him on securing his signature. In this particular case, the board decided that the secretary-manager should try to persuade the player to move from the East End to Fulham!

Proof that Stamford Bridge had quickly gained recognition from football's upper echelons was provided in March 1906 when the ground hosted the glamorous representative match that pitted the Football League against its Scottish counterpart.

From the regularity of the use of the Bridge for major sporting events in Chelsea's formative years, it seemed that Gus Mears's dream of making Stamford Bridge the major national stadium was becoming a reality.

7
PROMOTION

Playing for Chelsea is like theatre. You don't so much play as perform.

It's no good just lumping it about at Stamford Bridge; they expect something better.

Expectation is the start of anything good, anything worth having.

Eric Parsons (Chelsea, 1950–56)

1906/07

The Chelsea team continued to be a media fascination. A stop press section of a newspaper in those first years told the world that the Chelsea team 'are now enjoying a luncheon of roast mutton and dry toast'.

Following Chelsea's debut season, the club undertook a tour of Denmark, Vienna and Budapest. Copenhagen was overwhelmed 6-2, and the lively Pensioners went on to defeat the famous Hungarian League Champions Ferencváros. The Londoners had a programme of three games in the Austrian capital, beating Cricket Vienna (the side that would be Austria Wien) 3-1, First Vienna were thrashed 3-0 and a Wiener (Sport-Club) XI were totally outclassed in a 6-0 thumping. The experience whetted Jock Robertson's taste for continental football and following his stay at Chelsea he would return to Europe for a time to become one of the first British missionaries of the 'beautiful game'.

The 'baby Blues' started their second season in an optimistic mood that would prove to be well founded when the club achieved what must be considered one of their greatest accomplishments, winning promotion to the First Division of the Football League after just 76 games in the competition.

From the start of the season, Chelsea were once more up with the front runners and by the end of September only one point had been dropped in a 0–0 draw at Blackpool.

But behind the scenes there had been some degree of discontent. The board's relationship with Jock Robertson had grown increasingly strained. He had played in only three League games during the opening two months of the 1906/07 campaign, and appeared not to be totally committed to the club cause. Player absenteeism from training had been reported to the board on several occasions during the season. The club trainers kept an attendance book which was inspected by the board and on the basis of this £8 fines were administered to Robertson and Thomas McDermott for turning up for training inebriated. Jock had been particularly rowdy and, in answer to pleas for him to calm down, took to the heights of the East Stand in just his long-johns, hobnail boots and bowler hat to give a thunderous and protracted rendition of 'Scots Wha' Hae' that echoed loudly around the empty chasm of Stamford Bridge.

In November, player/secretary-manager Robertson

had his authority further undermined when a sub-committee consisting of Messrs HA Mears, EH Janes and FW Parker 'was appointed to apportion the work of the trainers, groundsman and others'.

When Robertson failed to attend the directors' meeting on 20 November, the secretary was asked to write to the secretary-manager requesting an explanation of his absence. A week later, a letter from Robertson arrived containing his resignation and a request for a free transfer.

Robertson's resignation was accepted and the free transfer approved on condition that he did not sign for a Football League Second Division side.

The notice to quit created some bad feeling and the chairman William Kirby received a letter (dated 30 November 1906) which he asked to be entered on the minutes – it read:

Dear Sir,
Knowing that Mr J. T. Robertson was no longer an official of the Chelsea F.C. I thought it my duty to inform you that he was in your office after 11 p.m. last Thursday Nov 29th.
Yours faithfully
H. Raucorn.

In January 1907, after 39 games and four goals, John Robertson was eventually signed (again as player/manager) by Glossop North End who were of course a Second Division club, after a certain amount of vacillation by the Chelsea board. Although he left the club in disgrace, the players Robertson had brought to Stamford Bridge would win the club promotion in April 1907.

Robertson would subsequently move to Old Trafford where he was the reserve-team manager from June 1909 to May 1910. He coached in Europe either side of World War I and was with Coventry City as a trainer for the 1927/28 season when the Sky Blues finished 20th out of 22 in the Third Division South. Jock died in Milton, Hampshire on 24 January 1935.

Lack of discipline among the players continued to be a problem. David Copeland, the club captain, was asked to report to the board meeting on 27 November. He turned up 'in a state of intoxication' and proceeded to hurl abuse at the directors. He left distraught and tearful, lamenting the departure of 'Jockey Robbo', claiming that without Robertson 'dare nay were be na club fer dee t'roon'. The board unanimously voted to suspend him for an unspecified (indefinite) period.

Copeland was instructed to send a letter of apology and was consequently asked to meet the board again on 11 December. At that meeting the board agreed to lift the suspension they had imposed on their skipper.

The run of bad news continued at Christmas when Scottish trainer Jimmy Miller suddenly died. He had played for his country during his time at Glasgow Rangers, scoring during each appearance (vs. England, 1897 and 1899). But Jim spent the majority of his 14-year playing career with Sunderland. During 1905/06, he played for Chelsea's reserves.

The New Year seemed to start well with League wins over Stockport County and Blackpool. However, after being held to a 2–2 draw in the first round of the FA Cup, Chelsea were beaten 1–0 at home by Lincoln City in the replay.

But, although away form had been erratic, consistency at Stamford Bridge had built a solid base for Chelsea's season. A fine run over Christmas – four away games without defeat – meant that by the turn of the year the West

Londoners had taken over the Division Two leadership from West Bromwich Albion, with 31 points from 20 games. This set up a relatively comfortable finish to the campaign.

On 8 April 1907, the famous comedian and music hall star George Robey organised a benefit game between Chelsea and a London All-Star XI side to provide some financial support for Jim Miller's wife. This led to Chelsea making a very odd bit of football history by signing Robey (who played for the Pensioners at inside-left during the benefit game and scored a decent goal) on amateur forms. He was registered to play for Chelsea in the club's London League fixtures but in fact he made just one appearance in the reserves, missing a goal from two yards out. 'I only joined Chelsea to keep them in the First Division,' he later quipped on stage. This started a long series of music-hall jokes with the club at the butt end that became something of a music-hall tradition. Of course, a hundred years later, most seem very hackneyed, for example,

A couple of chaps, Bert and Harry, are taking a stroll through Kensal Green Cemetery and they come across the headstone of a former mate of theirs that reads, 'HERE LIES FRED ATKINS, A GOOD MAN AND A CHELSEA SUPPORTER.'

Bert turns to Harry and asks, 'When did they start putting three fellers in one blinking grave?'

Or how about:

What does Gus Mears say when Chelsea score? 'Well done, men! Now let's have a go a getting a goal against our opponents.'

Chelsea did not surrender top place until early April when Nottingham Forest, who had beaten the home side 2–0 at Stamford Bridge at the beginning of February, pushed into the lead. By the time Gainsborough Trinity came to London for Chelsea's final home fixture on 27 April, they had achieved promotion. With the Division Two schedule complete, Leicester Fosse were nine points adrift of Chelsea's 57 points. This would be the most points the Pensioners would ever achieve up to the change from two to three points for a win in 1981.

In the end, the loss to Forest was the only home defeat of Chelsea's 19 (all the other games were victories – the side scored 55 goals and conceded just 10 at the Bridge) and it was Forest who eventually claimed the Championship, finishing just three points clear of Chelsea.

The promotion season had seen some interesting additions to the Stamford Bridge ranks. Bob Whiting had taken over from Mickey Byrne who had replaced Willie Foulke in goal. Willie would be a hard act to follow; his record of an unbroken sequence of nine clean sheets for Chelsea is unmatched to this day. He finished his official footballing career at Bradford City. Whiting was to prove almost as popular as Foulke had been with the Stamford Bridge crowd.

Other new faces included Scottish international wing-half George Henderson and Londoners Ted Birnie, from Crystal Palace, and the former West Ham player Billy Bridgeman. But the masterstroke in terms of acquisitions was persuading George 'Gatling Gun' Hilsdon to move from Upton Park in May 1906. The 19-year-old started his tenure in the ranks of the Blues in fine style by scoring five at the Bridge in the 9–2 season-opening game against Glossop North End, in the process silencing the criticism at the dropping of the popular centre-forward Frank Pearson. This would remain a record League win for the Pensioners.

On 16 February 1907, Hilsdon would become the first Chelsea player to be capped for England (he also got a hat-trick playing against the Irish League for the Football League). For five seasons, apart from one short break, he would be a consistent goalscorer for the embryonic Pensioners. Respected and feared by opponents everywhere, George's first term at the Bridge was a magnificent goal-laden campaign. Of the 80 goals Chelsea scored that season, Hilsdon netted 27. With the service of swift wingers Jimmy Frost and John Kirwan, the East Londoner was part of one of the most threatening forward lines in England at that time.

Skipper Bob McRoberts had proved to be a composed and reliable centre-half, while Joe Walton and Tommy Miller, as the side's regular full-backs throughout the season, had shown themselves to be a solid defensive pairing. Wing-halves George Henderson and the creative Ted

Birnie equipped themselves well behind inside-forwards Bridgeman and Jimmy Windridge, who with his close dribbling ball control delighted the supporters with his skill and some stunning goals. But the contribution of Whiting, who conceded just 34 goals all season, was a vital key to the Pensioners' success.

Chelsea as a club were growing to be part of the football establishment almost as quickly as their on-field achievements were taking them into the company of the finest in the game. Among the visitors to Stamford Bridge that season were the Prince and Princess of Wales, when they attended the annual fixture between the Army and the Royal Navy.

Although the price of a season ticket had risen, and although this would still be less than £2 for most, it was not cheap for an ordinary working person to attend football matches at this time. A craftsman could expect to earn around £1-10s and £2 a week and a general labourer might make between £70 and £80 a year (but many would need to work something like 60 hours a week to get this). However, compared to now, a football match was comparatively accessible entertainment and average gates were around 17,000 at the Bridge.

Chelsea had exceeded the hopes of the most optimistic of fans with the best goal difference in the League (+46).

In their moment of triumph, the Chelsea directors wanted to distinguish the club from their rivals and the stereotyped image of the game set by professional football's spiritual roots in the north. To record the achievement of the 1906/07 team, a meticulously staged and posed photograph was taken of the squad with a top hotel as a backdrop. The players were dressed in finely tailored three-piece suits, complete with fob-watch chains in their waistcoats, and their good haircuts were revealed by the lack of hats. There was not even the merest hint of the cloth-capped, woollen-muffled image associated with footballers of the time; Chelsea were 'Toffs'. But they were still obliged to look enviously at Northern teams dominating the greatest of all football trophies.

Everton once more made the Cup Final. But a crowd of 84,584 saw Sheffield Wednesday go 1–0 up after 21 minutes via a goal from Stewart. Sharp drew the Toffees level seven minutes before half-time but a last-minute goal from Simpson stopped the Liverpool Blues from becoming the first team since Blackburn Rovers in 1891 to retain the trophy. This was Wednesday's second Cup Final win. The first had been the 2-1 defeat of Wolverhampton Wanderers in 1896.

During their first two seasons of existence, Chelsea had caught the public imagination and almost everywhere the team went they achieved record gates. People were astonished at the Pensioners' confidence and many were envious as this rookie club reset the benchmarks of success that the majority of their peers had failed to approach during the history of League football. But most of the capital earned from this fame had been invested in the team. Accordingly, there had been little improvement made to the stadium apart from a billiards room, a club room and a couple of cycle sheds.

However, Stamford Bridge by this time had certainly taken over from the Crystal Palace in every respect except its seating capacity. Maybe Gus Mears should have taken the powerful hint sent his way during September 1906 when the Middlesex County Rugby Football Association (which had agreed terms to hire the Bridge to stage an England vs. South Africa international) walked out of negotiations and took the match to the Palace as there was not sufficient seating at Stamford Bridge.

8
GOALS FOR FUN

A lot of things get said about Chelsea, because people
seem to like talking about the club. But the club fits
where it is. Those two things are important. Because if
people are to value something firstly they have to feel
it's theirs and secondly other people need to be
interested in it.

Ron Greenwood (Chelsea, 1940–45 & 1952–55)

1907/08

Gus Mears had been realistic about his club's
prospects in the top flight of English football at
the start of the 1907/08 season; his words 'Now for
the struggle', uttered as he looked towards the first
game among the elite against proud Preston North

End, one of the great Lancastrian institutions of the early days of the game, were echoed, but with more than a hint of negativity, by the renowned CB Fry. Fry was probably the most exceptional all-round sportsman of the era and his view that Chelsea might not be able to live with the company the club were about to keep was seen by many as incontrovertible.

Changes were rung among the playing staff; remarkably, four joined their former manager Jock Robertson at Glossop North End.

Following Robertson's departure, William Lewis, the club secretary, took over the management of the team for six months in a 'caretaker' capacity, until David Calderhead, who was to remain the club's manager for more than a quarter of a century, took over in August 1907.

It had been in January 1907, in the first round of the previous season's FA Cup, that Calderhead's abilities first came to the attention of Chelsea officials. The Pensioners were drawn against the side the Scotsman would manage for seven years in all, Lincoln City. The Imps managed a 2–2 draw at Sincil Bank and four days later pulled off a victory at Stamford Bridge that could not fail to impress.

THE BIRTH OF THE BLUES

Born in the mining village of Hurlford, Dumfries (Ayrshire), on 19 June 1864, Calderhead was a man of few words and, while in charge of Chelsea, little was heard from him beyond the confines of Stamford Bridge. Not one for making forecasts about matches or indulging the press, his point of view was hardly ever expressed by way of newspaper columns or even in home programmes. This stance caused him to become known as the 'Chelsea Sphinx', suggesting awareness that Calderhead was more inclined to action than rhetoric. However, there were not many among his peers with a livelier penchant for the transfer market. In much the same way as Robertson had, Calderhead put together teams that attracted big crowds at a time when the money taken through the turnstiles was as much a definition of success as silverware.

A more than able and powerful centre-half in his playing days, he started his career in football with Queen of the South Wanderers, with whom he won a Scottish international cap (1889 vs. Ireland, Scotland won 7–0); he was the only player from the Dumfries club to represent Scotland.

Calderhead's international appearance attracted the attention of Notts County and he spent 10 years with them from 1889, making 278 League appearances, and was a member of County's FA Cup-winning side in 1894.

As Chelsea manager, Calderhead continued to sustain close links with the Scottish game and recruited players from all over Britain. After promotion, the Chelsea team-building strategy was spend, spend, spend, but, other than three promotions and a Cup during wartime, the investment failed to pay off.

Inside-forward Fred Rouse came to West London from Stoke City for a fee of £1,000 (the first four-figure signing for Chelsea, a tremendous amount of money in 1907) and other new recruits included Billy Brawn, Jimmy Stark, full-back Jack Cameron (who would be Chelsea's first Scottish international player in 1909 when he was selected for the side to meet England) and goalkeeper Jack Whitley. Calderhead had brought Jack with him from Lincoln and he would remain at Stamford Bridge as a player and trainer until May 1939. Ben Warren came from Derby County already an England international half-back. But his career would shortly be terminated by illness, prior to his death at the tragically young age of 38.

THE BIRTH OF THE BLUES

As November dawned, the gloomy forecasts made prior to the first ball of the season being kicked appeared completely reasonable. Chelsea were stranded at the bottom of the League having gained just three points from the possible 16 up for grabs over the eight games they had contested. Sheffield United and Manchester United had both hit four goals at Stamford Bridge, while Nottingham Forest had scored half-a-dozen against the travelling Pensioners.

But the biggest gate at any First Division match, vs. Woolwich Arsenal, took place on 9 November 1907; the takings were £1,626 and Chelsea won 2–1. This was the second of four successive home victories, alongside a 4–2 win at Deepdale, and Chelsea were hoisted five places from the foot of the table by Christmas so anxiety about possible relegation was lifting by the New Year.

Bob McRoberts, the club captain, moved from centre to right-half, with Ted Birnie operating on the opposite flank. This made room for Jimmy Stark at centre-half and, alongside full-back Jack Cameron in his partnership with Tommy Miller, the team put up a stronger level of resistance. Bob Whiting and Whitley shared the goalkeeping duties to make the West Londoners' defence begin to look effective.

George Hilsdon once more led the attack well enough to be awarded his first full England cap (against Northern Ireland). With Hilsdon's 24 goals, together with the contributions of inside-forwards Freddie Rouse and Jimmy Windridge, and Billy Brawn and Norman Fairgray (another signing from Lincoln City) on the wings, the attack looked much improved as the season matured.

One of the most notable matches of the 1907/08 season was in the first round proper (the equivalent to the third round today) of the 'English Cup' (11 January 1907). Chelsea's tie against Worksop Town was transferred to Stamford Bridge officially at the request of the Nottinghamshire side, but it had been the Chelsea directors who had convinced their Worksop equivalents to ask for the game to be moved to Stamford Bridge on the somewhat doubtful premise that 'we have only one First League match at home between Boxing Day and the third week in February'.

It is pretty certain that the financial advantages of the transfer would have been a big consideration for Worksop and almost 19,000 paid at the Stamford Bridge turnstiles to watch a match.

The line-up for the match was:

CHELSEA: Jack Whitley; Jock Cameron, Augustus Harding, George Henderson, Jimmy Stark, Ted Birnie, Billy Brawn, Ben Whitehouse, George Hilsdon, Jimmy Windridge, Billy Bridgeman

WORKSOP TOWN: Fern; Coupe, Gregory, Parramore, Walters, Westwood, Cooke, Richardson, Padley, Walker, Bale

It is fair to say that the game itself was pretty much one-way traffic, as one scribe of the time recorded, 'The emotions of the crowd were never stirred.' However, it might have been different had Worksop taken the scoring chance they had in the first 60 seconds. But the shock of that near thing seemed to steel the home side's focus and they swiftly dominated the encounter.

Goals from George Hilsdon, Jimmy Windridge (2) and Billy Bridgeman in the first 45 minutes gave Chelsea a lead that looked to have more or less finished the game. But the Tigers, living up to that nickname, tried to fight back and their efforts were rewarded when their inside-forward and skipper Richardson pulled one back for the Midland League side.

That goal was not to be the start of a revival, although, showing huge courage and pride, Worksop toiled to give the scoreline some respectability; Padley, the visitors' centre-forward, hit the bar and their inside-left Walker missed a relatively simple opportunity to score.

Hilsdon was to add three to Chelsea's total in the five minutes after the resumption, a fantastic feat, but it was achieved while the Worksop left-half was off the field having an injury tended. However, Hilsdon's shots from long range tore into the net like avenging banshees. He was to score another brace before the referee, Mr JW Bailey from Leicester, blew the final whistle, but it was only Fern's bravery in the visitors' goal that prevented Hilsdon and Chelsea getting into double figures.

The 'Gatling Gun' man had scored more goals in one game than any other Chelsea player was ever to manage, a record that stands to this day.

There was some solace for Worksop by way of

their share of the gate; £381-10s-2d was a good day for them and far in excess of what they would have made if the tie had been staged at their Central Avenue ground, about £300 more.

Given such a convincing victory, it is perhaps surprising that Chelsea were not entirely satisfied with the day. Announcing that it was ridiculous to propose that the choice of ground might have had an impact on the outcome of the game, one Chelsea official further claimed that, but for a reluctance to take too many chances on the frozen ground, the home side might have hit a score or more goals. He then censured what he saw as Worksop's 'none too clean methods in stopping', and drew notice to an exceptionally nasty foul inflicted on Hilsdon, declaring, 'Instant ordering off is the only proper treatment for the football hooligan.'

Unfortunately, Calderhead's men could not come close to replicating their feat in the next round, where they suffered a 1–0 defeat at Old Trafford.

Wolverhampton Wanderers got to the FA Cup Final for the fourth time that year and won it for the first time since 1893. In front of a crowd of 74,697, goals from England international the

Reverend Kenneth Reginald Gunnery Hunt five minutes before half-time and George Hedley two minutes later more or less killed the game, but Newcastle kept fighting and seemed to have given themselves hope in the 73rd minute when Jimmy Howie halved the deficit. However, Billy Harrison settled matters with five minutes of the game remaining.

On 8 February, a Rugby League Test match between what was then known as the Northern Union and New Zealand was staged at Stamford Bridge; the Kiwis won 18–6.

Having averaged more than a point a game for the last six months of the season, Chelsea ended their campaign in 13th place in Division One, by no means the catastrophe that had been predicted by not a few 'educated' commentators of the time. In fact, the Pensioners were only bettered by one Southern club (Bristol City in 10th) and finished above Arsenal (who concluded the term in 14th position). That said, Bolton Wanderers were relegated with 33 points and Manchester United, who won the Championship for the first time that season, pulled in a total of 52 points.

9

UNPREDICTABLE ENTITY

You've got to have a passion for something,
even if it's an old football team. Is having no passion
for anything better?

Peter Houseman (Chelsea, 1962–65)

1908/09

On the last Saturday in September, Chelsea were sitting in fourth place, but their season seemed to be blown apart by the winter winds. When Stamford Bridge played host to Bristol City for the penultimate game of the 1908/09 campaign, it was still possible for Chelsea to be relegated. Leicester Fosse were doomed, but Bradford City were within two points of the West Londoners, who had an inferior goal average.

The 3–1 win over the Robins and three days later a 1–0 victory over Fosse allowed Chelsea to finish in a place that did not exactly reflect the disappointing nature of their performance over the season. Chelsea's second season in the First Division was just a bit more successful than the first. With one more point they improved by two places to finish 11th in the League. The club had hung on to their First Division status, but the promise of an excellent start to the season which probably motivated Chelsea's unprecedented programme sales at the League match, vs. Villa, on 26 September, with takings of £97-3s-9d, had not been fulfilled. That season saw another programme record for Chelsea; over the campaign the club sold 278,878 copies at a gross value of £1,161-19s-10d.

Yet again, the FA Cup campaign had been short-lived. The second-round exit at the hands of Blackburn Rovers after the defeat of Hull City following a replay at Stamford Bridge was hardly the stuff of dreams.

But six-times England international Ben Warren

had arrived at the Bridge from Derby County to make a swift impact at right-half. Gaining four more caps during the season, Ben was a model professional on and off the pitch and was called 'the best wing-half in the kingdom' by the sports writers of the day; he was also said to be 'worth three men to his side'.

With the exception of Bob McRoberts sharing the centre-half role with Ted Birnie, who sometimes played at left-half, the defence was much the same as the previous season. Custodian Jack Whitley was regularly protected by full-backs Jack Cameron and Tommy Miller.

George Hilsdon took his Chelsea goal account to 76 in 99 League games and, apart from Fred Rouse making way for Percy Humphreys at inside-right, the attack was unchanged; the wingers were Billy Brawn and Norman Fairgray while Jimmy Windridge once more habitually covered inside-left. During the 1908/09 term, Windridge's constantly outstanding performances from the first days of Chelsea's history were recognised with his selection for the England team, along with Warren and Hilsdon. This trio gained a total of 20 caps during that season.

However, while Chelsea were achieving a reputation for fielding players of individual brilliance, they were also beginning to be seen as an unpredictable entity. The official Hull City programme for the first-round FA Cup tie on Humberside told how 'Chelsea are one of the most brilliant and, at the same time, one of the most disappointing teams in the First Division. Individually, the side is for the most part composed of "star performers". There is no team in the League with a finer forward line – on paper. Still, they do not make headway in the League table.'

Newcastle United won their second League Championship, finishing a comfortable seven points clear of Everton. Manchester City (with just three points less than Chelsea) and Leicester Fosse were relegated.

Manchester United defeated Bristol City in the FA Cup Final at Crystal Palace. The 71,401 spectators got just one goal for their troubles, a 22nd-minute effort from Sandy Turnbull. This was the first of United's 11 Cup wins.

But there was at least something to bring a smile to football fans' faces around SW6 that season when the England Amateur Football team defeated their Dutch counterparts 9–1 at the Bridge on 11 December 1908.

10
RELEGATION

*In football (as in life) success or failure is always going
to depend on how well you prepare to meet the
unexpected rather than how big or impressive your plans
are or what they say about what you expect.*

Edward Joseph Drake (Chelsea manager, 1952–61)

1909/10

Chelsea's continuing struggle to establish
themselves as an influential First Division club
saw the side keep themselves just clear of the
dreaded drop zone for most of the season and this
seemed to be appreciated by the fans, as
evidenced by the crowd of 70,000 that came to
Stamford Bridge to watch Newcastle United

defeated on 27 December. This was the largest ever attendance at an English League game. The Chelsea programme called it 'phenomenal' and of course it was, but the next few months were to be anticlimactic to say the least. For the best part of the season, poor form away from Stamford Bridge was to be crucial and from a stage in the season where 38 points were possible the Pensioners were to gain just eight.

However, it has to be said that, from the initial match of the League campaign (a 2–2 home draw with Nottingham Forest), fortune did not favour the boys in blue. Injuries were a constant and the notion of sending a full-strength team out to do battle, or even establish a settled side, appeared to be beyond Chelsea. Although the era was one wherein squads were the size of brigades, the use of 34 players in the League side during the season demonstrated the depth of woe at the Bridge. Calderhead failed to establish a winning combination, but it seemed things just fell apart as the reliable performers of the previous two campaigns – the likes of defender Ted Birnie and forwards George Hilsdon and Norman Fairgray – missed over half the club's games. But the prolonged absence of Ben Warren through injury was probably the cruellest of blows.

Hilsdon's three goals from 15 matches (he had been out for nearly half the season through injury) seemed a paltry total compared to successive tallies of 27, 24 and 25 in the three terms prior to the 1909/10 season, and for many this was a decisive factor in the demise of Chelsea; the club simply had no replacement for his knack of finding the rigging.

The enforced blooding of players was a season-long saga, a number of whom would become famous under the Blue banner. Ball-wizard Marshall McEwan, defenders Walter Bettridge and Fred Taylor all made their first-team debuts, as did the hard-shooting inside-forward Bob Whittingham (a native of the Potteries) and the imposing centre-half Alec Ormiston. These men were destined to play major roles in Chelsea's future.

The celebrated Corinthian amateur centre-forward VJ (Vivian) Woodward also started his long association with the Bridge. An upstanding Kennington-born 'gentleman player', whose neat blazers were the finishing touch to his dapper style, Viv was an amateur footballer by calling and an architect by profession. In the years preceding World War I, Woodward, who had arrived at Stamford Bridge from Tottenham as an emergency signing at a time when Chelsea had 17 players on the injury list, forged a destructive partnership with Windridge and, with Hilsdon, they formed an all-English international inside trio. Woodward's ability to hold the ball and run long distances, despite the attentions of defenders, marked him out as one of the great players of his era. He had left Tottenham for the wonderfully Corinthian motive of preferring the shorter journey to Stamford Bridge from his home than the excursion across town to suburban-based Spurs.

During April, in a desperate effort to avoid relegation, five new players were brought to the club at a cost of £3,575, a sum that is a (relative) match for any to be paid out in the future; a result of this attempt by Chelsea to spend their way out of trouble motivated the Football League to subsequently introduce the 16 March transfer 'deadline', after which date players could only represent their new clubs with the consent of the FA management committee. The transfers had to be cleared by the fourth Thursday of March at

3 p.m. and after that the FA could influence the deals by, for instance, allowing players to play only League matches. It seems the Pensioners had a reputation as big spenders long before the arrival of Russian cash.

The injection of skill and talent in the long term was to pay dividends but it could not stop what in the end felt like Chelsea's inevitable fall back to the Second Division, that had appeared likely several times after the club's first promotion in 1907. The Pensioners' fortunes were more or less settled at White Hart Lane when the home side won 2–1 after a titanic battle. Ironically, Percy Humphreys, who had departed Stamford Bridge in December, slotted home the winning goal for Spurs.

It was scant consolation but at least the club had avoided finishing rock bottom (newly promoted Bolton Wanderers, on 24 points, lagged five points behind the Londoners) and Woolwich Arsenal were just a point better than the men from the Bridge. Aston Villa won the Championship (for the sixth time but it was their first title since 1900) five points clear of Liverpool.

Chelsea fared little better in the FA Cup,

continuing their tradition of an early exit, when, having defeated Hull City 2–1 at the Bridge, they allowed Tottenham to beat them in SW6 by the only goal of the game. Curiously, Hull drew nearly 3,000 more spectators than London neighbours Spurs (34,700).

Newcastle met Barnsley in the Final at Crystal Palace where 76,980 fans, after Harry Tufnell scored eight minutes before half-time, watched as the Tykes looked like making their first Final a winning one. But with seven minutes to play England international Jock Rutherford forced extra-time, which ended goalless, and the game was replayed at Goodison Park. Two penalties from Albert Shepherd (another England man) in the 52nd and 62nd minute without reply ended the Yorkshiremen's hopes.

But the season saw yet another Chelsea player receive international recognition; in 1910 Wales capped Evan Jones, their first Chelsea player, who would play twice for his country facing Scotland and Ireland.

Chelsea's first relegation was the only setback the Pensioners had experienced in their short history. International calls had deprived the team of an effective strike force for long periods and this had much to do with the club achieving only 11 wins in their 38 games. How they would handle their biggest disappointment thus far was probably one of the biggest tests the club would face for many a decade.

11
GLORIOUS FAILURE

Almost! But in football, almost is nothing!

Jose Mourinho (Chelsea manager, 2004–07)

1910/11

Chelsea started their sixth season feeling unlucky to be back in the Second Division, particularly as the club had made a string of new signings during the previous term. But the side continued to be reinforced, with goalkeeper Jim ('Moly') Molyneux coming from Stockport County as cover for Jack Whitley. Jim impressed during the practice games and as such was selected for the opening match of Chelsea's campaign, the aim of which was to bounce straight back into the top flight. It was a good start; a 4–1 victory at the Baseball Ground was a result few would match at the home of the Rams that term. Molyneux was to miss just one match in the League that season (21 January, vs. Leicester Fosse at Stamford Bridge) and that was the result of injury rather than form.

As the season progressed, Frederick Parker's frustration was hardly camouflaged in a lampoon of journalists and officials of rival teams in the *Chelsea Chronicle*. He was tired of the way Chelsea were depicted and criticised seemingly at every turn. In a piece entitled the 'Philosophical Pensioner', he wrote of a fictional conversation between a son and his dad. The father told his boy that not everyone likes to 'kick a man when he is down': 'If you knew human nature, my son, you would understand that you cannot gather the flowers of sympathy in the garden of those who double-bolted the garden against you. Nor can you expect their own particular scribes to look beyond their noses for an excuse for your calamity. They write, "The Pensioner with all his money bags could not save himself from the doom of the Second Division." Never a word of the accidents and illnesses which incapacitated nearly a third of my whole team.'

Parker (taking the part of the Pensioner) then turned to accusations about the club's habit of spending big money on player transfers: 'Some there were who unburdened themselves in reams over "the power of the purse", forgetful of the fact that my purse was made and filled by my friends and supporters. It was my duty to these friends and supporters to expend the money which they made for me in their interests. I had more followers than any club in London ... I did not spend my cash. I assure you, for the mere fun of enriching other clubs ... Chelsea has never been sweet to the ears of those who prophesied and hoped for my failure.'

It seems some things never change.

Chelsea were never out of touch with the leaders throughout the season and at the start of February were in second place in the table, a position that they were to hold until the final home fixture against Burnley; Chelsea were level with Bolton Wanderers on goal average and two points behind leaders West Bromwich Albion.

The Clarets were defeated 3–0, but, having to cope with a heavy injury list, fielding walking wounded, the Pensioners' last away matches against Bolton and the struggling Gainsborough Trinity both ended in defeat for Chelsea and the prize of promotion was lost.

However, the 1910/11 season saw Chelsea make their first real impact in the FA Cup with the club reaching the semi-final stage. On 14 January, it had taken a replay to eliminate Leyton but the West Londoners brushed Chesterfield Town aside in the next round to set up a meeting with Wolverhampton Wanderers at Molineux. The all-Second Division tie was a hard-fought and exciting match in which Chelsea were reduced to 10 men for the last 30 minutes after Sam Downing was injured, as at this time substitutes were not allowed in English League games. (In fact, this would not change until the 1965/66 season, and the first-ever Chelsea substitute was John Boyle who came on for George Graham on 28 March 1965 during Chelsea's 3–0 victory over Fulham at Craven Cottage.) But the 2–0 win brought Swindon Town, then a Southern League side, to the Bridge where they were beaten 3–1 to the delight of the record 77,952 crowd (at that point, the highest attendance for any FA Cup tie outside the Final); no Chelsea match would attract more fans until 12 March 1935 when 82,905 turned up to watch the 1–1 draw with Arsenal.

Newcastle United stood between Chelsea and a place in the FA Cup Final, but at St Andrew's, Birmingham, the Pensioners were well beaten (3–0) by the good First Division side. The Magpies went on to meet first-time finalists Bradford City at Crystal Palace where 69,098 fans witnessed the goalless Final. The replay at Old Trafford saw Scottish international Jimmy Speirs score on the quarter-of-an-hour mark and this was enough to take the Cup to Yorkshire.

One football scribe called Chelsea's season 'a glorious failure' and the Pensioners' campaign was, in the end, a tale of 'so near yet so far'. A Cup Final and promotion double or even claiming 'the English Cup' and the Second Division Championship had been possible. There were those that were to claim that the commitment to playing a highly entertaining game had cost the club dear, that more negative tactics would have taken Chelsea further still. However, that debate is always with us.

Third in the Second Division, with Whittingham (38 goals) and Hilsdon (18) forming a lethal spearhead, was not enough to win promotion. The Chelsea cause was not helped by a number of acts of indiscipline on the part of the players in the pubs of Fulham and Hammersmith, but the club's popularity had increased and it had been a landmark season at Stamford Bridge.

There were some who believed that the FA Cup run that took the Blues to the semi-finals for the first time had deflected Chelsea's push for promotion that had failed by just two points (West Bromwich Albion had gone up as Champions with a total of 53 points, Bolton Wanderers were two points behind them), but at the Annual General Meeting Chairman Kirby declared, 'It is not the policy of the Chelsea directors to tell our players not to try to win any competition we enter.'

During the campaign, Bob Whittingham, whose incredibly powerful shooting had made his a name to be feared, George Hilsdon and the intelligent and skilful Vivian Woodward had shown themselves to be arguably the strongest inside forward trio in the English game. On the wings, Angus Douglas (who would be capped by Scotland in 1911 – he was in the side that defeated Ireland 2-0; Chelsea did not produce another Scottish international until 1928 when Tommy Law was selected to face England) and Marshall McEwan were regulars, while right-half Ben Warren (who was once more capped by England) continued to be 'Mr Reliable', with Sam Downing covering left-half. English McConnell, young David Calderhead (the manager's son) and Alec Ormiston shared the centre-half duties.

Full-back Walter Bettridge also caught the eye. He was one of the first players in his position to 'overlap' down the touchline, reinforcing the attack. His buccaneering raids were complemented by Jack Cameron, who on the left stood solid in his defensive duties.

In the *Chelsea Chronicle*, Fred Parker wrote, 'There is a 7lb coke-hammer waiting for the next idiot who asks a Chelsea official, "Why didn't you go up last season?"'

12
BACK WITH THE BIG BOYS

When I first heard about Viagra, I thought it was a new
player Chelsea had just signed.

The late Tony Banks, Baron of Stratford, Labour MP

and Chelsea supporter (1943–2006)

1911/12

Up to 1911, Chelsea appeared to be maturing into
a side that were too good for the Second Division,
but not good enough for a permanent place in the
top flight and the 1911/12 season seemed to
confirm this limbo status.

Early in January, the Blues moved into second
place in the table but had been thereabouts from
the start of the campaign and were being seen as

a side ripe for promotion in more than a few quarters and it was at the Bridge that they laid the foundation for this view. But on 24 February something of the reality of things was literally brought home when the Division leaders Burnley won 2–0 in West London. Stamford Bridge had not been the site of a Chelsea League defeat for almost two years (on 28 March 1910 Woolwich Arsenal had crossed London to defeat the Pensioners by the only goal of the game).

It was also in February (4th) that the club founder Gus Mears passed away. The 'father of the club' had suffered from blood poisoning as a result of chronic kidney failure. He died at his home, 390 Upper Richmond Road, and was buried in Brompton Cemetery, within earshot of roars from the Bridge; he was just 39 years of age. His passing was a sad loss not only to Stamford Bridge and Chelsea but also to football in general. His popularity was evidenced by an attendance of more than 300 at his funeral, even though it was pouring with rain. The cortege included a hearse, a flower hearse and seven carriages. The procession halted for a moment outside the entrance to Stamford Bridge.

In his fine waistcoats, Mears had a rotund figure that made him look older than his years. He liked the good things his wealthy lifestyle could give him, but these may have helped contribute to his death. Football was his passion, although his fellow directors might, at times, have wished him to have been a bit less argumentative. He had something of a cavalier attitude to life but conversely could also be a calming influence when needed. He was fond of saying 'Don't worry' and dealt with everything from press attacks to setbacks for the team via this mantra. This was part of his good-humoured indifference that had the power to put things in perspective.

The *Chelsea Chronicle* lamented the club's loss, telling how Mears's curt yet composed demeanour camouflaged a kind man, and described his love of Stamford Bridge and its football team. It went on, 'He has left behind him a monument that is more eloquent than any carved epitaph. In the Chelsea Football Club and the Stamford Bridge Sports Ground which he gave to the sport-loving masses of London, his memory will remain green so long as the Chelsea ground shall exist.'

However, football has a life of its own and it

seems to outlive us all, even the most influential and historic figures and powerful ideals. That, in a way, is a comfort to us who call ourselves supporters; we are part of the breath of something immortal.

Claude Kirby, chairman of the club and an old friend of the Mears family, looked to continue the traditions his pal Gus had set in place, but he did not have the same financial connections, influence and authority of the club's founder.

Early in April at the Baseball Ground, Derby County took over second position as the Pensioners were hit by another 2–0 result. The Rams were then four points behind Burnley.

A perfect record over Easter and a crucial victory at Barnsley kept Chelsea in contention but everything now depended on the last day of the season when Bradford Park Avenue came to Stamford Bridge to contest what was to be a hard-fought game.

The Pensioners needed to defeat the Stans at the Bridge to ensure the season would conclude with promotion for the SW6 men, but Burnley were level with Chelsea in second place. If both Chelsea and Burnley were victorious, then goal average would be the deciding factor. However, a demanding League schedule that had obliged Chelsea to contest three matches over just five days would have taken its toll on the home team.

The Chelsea side that ran out against the Clarets on that day late in April included Jim Molyneux, Wally Bettridge, who his manager called 'the pluckiest little player that ever pulled on a football boot', Billy Cartwright, Fred Taylor, Alec Ormiston, Jack Harrow, Angus Douglas, Bob Whittingham, Viv Woodward, Charlie Freeman and Billy Bridgeman.

Although the match was one of those anxious encounters that were to characterise Chelsea over the years, the crowd of 40,000 lifted their team and in the 32nd minute Whittingham laid on a first goal for Charlie Freeman, who would be part of the Chelsea training staff until 1946, but had not been a regular choice for the first XI during the 1911/12 campaign. It was the only goal of the game, but enough to win the West Londoners promotion as Burnley (who would finish two points behind Chelsea) went down 2–0 in Wolverhampton to the Wanderers.

At the final whistle of the season, the supporters

invaded the Stamford Bridge pitch and thousands massed in front of the stand to celebrate the club's return to the First Division.

Chelsea and Derby County went up level on 54 points, but the Rams had a better goal average and so claimed the Championship.

The FA Cup once more became the short-lived dream it had been for most of Chelsea's brief history. A more than creditable victory over Division One side Sheffield United at the Bridge was followed by a 2-0 defeat away to Bradford City. Barnsley made their second Final, meeting West Bromwich Albion at Crystal Palace. The crowd was a relatively modest 54,556. There were no goals after extra-time so there was a replay at Bramall Lane. With two minutes of extra-time remaining, Harry Tufnell scored to keep the Cup in Yorkshire.

With 57 goals from 73 games, the battling centre-forward Bob Whittingham had been a vital element in the Pensioners' attack force. He was a war horse in the penalty area. Brought to Stamford Bridge from Bradford City in 1909 for a fee of £1,300, his 26 League strikes in that promotion season made Whittingham a man to be feared by goalkeepers, with his reputation for forcing his way through and driving in splendid goals from long distances causing one to remark, 'I would rather face his Satanic majesty than Whittingham.'

Bob Thomson concluded the season among the first-choice strikers while Angus Douglas and Billy Bridgeman (a very valuable player who adapted to several forward roles over the years) were the flankmen. George Dodd also made significant contributions.

As is always the way in football, as new players were shining through, the old guard had to make way and at the Bridge in 1911 two men left an indelible mark in the Chelsea chronicles. The English international wing-half Ben Warren was already suffering from the infirmity that would cause his early death, and George Hilsdon, seemingly unable to control his weight, became progressively more prone to injury and as such was finding it hard to hold down a place in the side. But George will always be the first in a long line of brilliant and high-scoring Chelsea centre-forwards.

By this time, several players whose longevity of service at Stamford Bridge would provide the basis of the future of the club had joined the side. From Croydon Common, Jack Harrow, a defender in the Chopper Harris mould, started his 15-year playing career. He would play for the Football League vs. the Southern League in 1914 and almost equal his years of playing service as a member of the training staff. And Jim Molyneux was to be custodian of the Chelsea rigging for a dozen seasons including those during World War I. His goalkeeping deputy, Jack Whitley, was a Blue for 32 years, mostly as first-team trainer.

Walter Bettridge and Jack Cameron had continued their successful full-back partnership. Wing-half Fred Taylor would play for the Football League vs. Southern League in 1909.

Bob Thomson, an import from Croydon Common, was a burly forward and famously one-eyed, but Bob lived with his disability using his seemingly innate Cockney sense of humour. When questioned about his handicap once, Thomson allegedly said, 'When the ball is coming my way I shut the other eye and play from memory.' When asked by secretary-manager Calderhead, 'How do you manage, Bob, when the ball comes to you on your blind side?' Thomson was reputed to have replied, 'I just shut the other eye and bundle into the nearest back.'

However, Vivian Woodward, although having been confined to just 14 League appearances, with his sportsmanship, boyish good looks, Corinthian manners and temperance (in contrast, at that point in time to one Chelsea player who, while drunk, had been suspended for knocking out a cab horse) had been inspirational. He was the greatest amateur striker of his day and, although not a tall man, barely medium height and slightly built, he was a brilliant dribbler and packed a powerful shot that brought him a plethora of goals over the years. He once netted half-a-dozen for England in a massacre of Holland and it was agreed that he was among his nation's finest ever centre-forwards. Philip Noel-Baker, the diplomat and Labour MP, called Woodward 'the living embodiment of the finest spirit of the game'.

Known to his friends as Jack, Woodward captained Great Britain to the gold medal at the 1912 Olympics and he is believed to have set the standard of fair play and gentlemanliness that was to be understood as an integral part of English football up to the last quarter of the 20th century.

Although Woodward grew up in Clacton, he was born in London. His father had an enduring dislike of football, which was not tempered when his son became the target of some of the excesses of the primeval defending of the early era of the game. However, Viv never succumbed to the temptation of retaliation and to a great extent avoided serious injury. When asked about his treatment at the hands of some of the renowned butchers of the day, he would refer to the presence of the referee and his faith in the officials to manage affairs. His skill and utter Englishness were very much the standard and attitude that Chelsea as a club wanted to foster and make synonymous with their name. This was probably one aim that was never truly realised.

13
ON THE BRINK

He said, 'Chelsea like to get forward.' Who don't
like to get forward? What team likes to go backward ...
Apart from Arsenal?

Tommy Docherty (Chelsea manager, 1967–75)

1912/13

Chelsea manager David Calderhead had put together debatably the strongest side the club had known, but the team struggled to adapt to the demands of Division One football. George Hilsdon had left Stamford Bridge and returned to Upton Park. His 107 goals in 164 games, between 1906 and 1912, placed him seventh in the list of Chelsea's all-time top scorers in 2008. Hilsdon's

strike partner Whittingham stood equal with
Gianfranco Zola as 13th highest-scoring Blue in
history; Whittingham hit the rigging 80 times in
129 games and it took Zola 312 outings to match
his total. But Whittingham found the defences of
the ilk of Sunderland and Aston Villa more
challenging than those arrayed against him by the
likes of Leeds City and Gainsborough Trinity.

The rear-guard thrown up by Chelsea fared little
better; only relegated Woolwich Arsenal conceded
more goals.

On Christmas Day 1912, Manchester United
inflicted a 4–1 defeat on the home side at
Stamford Bridge; this was the 12th loss, including
a five-game run without a single Blue goal, of
Chelsea's season (it was the 19th game of the term)
and the club were stuck in 18th position
throughout the five months to the end of the
campaign. A really low point was 29 March when
Blackburn Rovers inflicted what would stand as a
record home defeat for Chelsea: 6–1. This was as
bad as it got until Notts County hit half-a-dozen
without reply at Stamford Bridge in the 1923/24
relegation season.

If the 1912/13 season had not ended with three

successive victories, there could be little doubt that the West Londoners would have been on their way back to the Second Division.

Defender George Hunter and Celtic left-winger John Brown, who had been imported into the ranks of the Blues in March, played a big part in Chelsea holding on to their Division One status. Goalkeeping duties were shared between amateur Ron Brebner (another new signing) and Jim Molyneux. North-Easterner Brebner was a dental surgeon by profession but got his teeth into the job of being the last line of defence at the Bridge and was one of the best of the net custodians of his time, being awarded 23 amateur caps for England. Along with fellow Pensioner Viv Woodward, he was also a member of the British Olympic gold medal-winning side in the Stockholm Games of 1912.

During the season, Jimmy Sharp took over Jock Cameron's full-back role to make a regular pairing with Walter Bettridge, while Harry Ford, a native of Fulham and a former pupil of King's Road School, began his long career at outside-right. Harry stood just 5' 7" but was quite often one of the tallest in the Pensioners' front line.

Chelsea's most obvious deficit was a reliable goalscorer. Bob Whittingham, who had amassed 56 goals over the two previous seasons, had only hit the back of the net seven times by the end of April, while Vivian Woodward had scored 10 goals.

Again, the FA Cup felt like a bit of a rerun of previous seasons for Chelsea. Southend United headed back east after the first-round tie on the back of a 5–2 defeat that included a couple of wildly contested penalties.

In the next round, a Chelsea forward was twice hacked down by seemingly rabid Sheffield Wednesday defenders as he made a clear run into the penalty area. But no foul was awarded. The 1–1 draw at the Bridge set up a replay wherein the ominous Owls slaughtered the unhappy Londoners 6–0 at Hillsborough, the biggest ever loss in the Cup for the Blues.

Aston Villa won the trophy in the 75th minute of the game at Crystal Palace. The huge 121,919 crowd roared in approval as Tommy Barber sank Sunderland in the Black Cats' first-ever Final appearance.

With 28 points, Chelsea ended the season five points clear of Notts County who accompanied

Woolwich Arsenal on the relegation trail. Sunderland won the Championship with 54 points. It was the Wearsiders' fifth title but the first for 11 years.

Also in 1913 Tom Hewitt played three times for Wales in all their Home International games. He would be the last Chelsea man to win a Welsh cap until 1963 when Graham Moore was selected for the side to play Brazil.

But, despite a near-ignominious season for the team, the ground itself was faring rather well. Stamford Bridge was still pulling in the punters, and England's win over Scotland on 5 April 1913 (the first of three pre-World War II internationals to be staged at the stadium) was watched by a crowd of 52,000, Aston Villa's 'Happy' Harry Hampton, the 'Wellington Whirlwind', scoring the only goal of the game. Receipts of £1,900 were recorded on Good Friday when Aston Villa came to the Bridge setting up a new record for a League match at Chelsea – £600 more than the income generated from programme sales for the entire season.

14
NOT HALF
TOP HALF

Football is about glory, it is about doing things
in style and with a flourish, about going out and beating
the lot, not waiting for them to die of boredom.

Danny Blanchflower (Chelsea manager, 1978–79)

1913/14

When Preston North End arrived at the Bridge on 4 October, the initial five League games had provided only one point for bottom club Chelsea. Although the 2–0 win over the visitors was followed by a 1–0 defeat at St James' Park, three consecutive victories followed: a 3–0 result against Liverpool at the Bridge; a 2–1 win at Villa

Park and the 3–2 defeat of Middlesbrough in London. This was the start of a Blue revival which helped the Pensioners navigate their way out of the relegation zone.

Founded on good form at Stamford Bridge, respectable mid-table life was the story of the rest of the season. In nine home games between October and February, Chelsea dropped just two points.

But, again, the Pensioners failed to make any impression in the Cup. Injuries sustained during a fierce battle at the Den made Chelsea's prospects for the replay four days later look unpromising. At the Bridge on 14 January, after being reduced to 10 men before the game was even a quarter over, things looked even more grim as the Lions held on to a single-goal lead, defying the run of play. A total of £2,700 in gate money over the two games did not compensate for elimination by the Southern League jam makers, a club that would not be elected to the Football League until 1920 when they became a founding member of the Third Division South.

The Cup Final at Crystal Palace would be contested between two first-time finalists, Burnley and Liverpool. The Clarets won 1–0, thanks to England international Bert Freeman's goal 13 minutes into the second half.

Again, this season, Stamford Bridge itself was doing quite well. On Tuesday, 24 February 1914, representatives of New York and Chicago baseball teams attended the Chelsea board meeting, looking to stage a baseball match at Stamford Bridge just two days later (the stadium was one of the few arenas in the UK big enough to stage the game). There was agreement that the Americans would hire the ground for £30 plus expenses and so on the 26th the New York Giants played the Chicago White Sox in SW6 as the finale of their 1913/14 World Tour. This would not be the last time that the Fulham Road would play host to the great American passion.

It was during this season that inside-right Harold Halse came to West London from Aston Villa to start his long and distinguished career at the Bridge. He teamed up with centre-forward Bob Thomson. Adding skill and elegance to the side, he finished the campaign as the club's top scorer. A Leyton boy, gifted with a thunderously powerful shot, Halse had won an FA Cup winners medal with the Villans in 1913. Halse would be selected to play for the Football League in 1913 and 1914.

Centre-half Tommy Logan, from Falkirk, became a regular for the side and the orderly wing-half/half-back Nils 'the Great Dane' Middelboe also came into the first team and this duo noticeably bolstered the defence. Standing a lithe 6' 2", the Dane had a stride that covered yards, but he was an intelligent player and used the ball well, which at that time was not a common quality in a defender. A popular member of the team, Middelboe had played in the 1908 Olympics Games in London; his country was defeated in the final by Great Britain. However, on 19 October 1908, he achieved the historic distinction of being the first player ever to score in an Olympic Games, against France.

Nils was also selected for the Games in 1912 in Stockholm where he captained Denmark and once more he went to the final to again lose to Great Britain.

The Dane was not the first overseas player to turn out for Chelsea. The German-born (1884) Max Seeburg holds that distinction, having played for the Pensioners' reserve team in 1906. (The

Chelsea Chronicle detailed him as 'Seeberg'.) During World War I, Seeburg was interned at Newbury for a short time; he had wrongly believed he was 'naturalised', but he was detained even though his father, Franck, was fighting for the British Army.

And, in fact, on 6 November 1905, a crowd of 3,000 turned out to watch a Chelsea side that boasted just one Englishman, Frank Pearson, in a friendly against First Division Everton. That day the Pensioners fielded a mixture of 10 Scots and Irish players.

Three Indian-born players were on Chelsea's books prior to the arrival of Middelboe, but all had British backgrounds: Charles Donaghy, Hugh Dolby and George Hunter. Donaghy, who joined Chelsea in 1905, was born in 1890 in Dalhousie, Fort William, in the Himalayas. His father was an Irish sergeant in the British Army and his mother was from Lancashire. Signed by Chelsea in February 1913, 'Cocky' Hunter was born in Peshawar. Audacious and a tad unruly, he turned out for the first team but joined Manchester United for £1,300. In World War I, he was recruited to the secret service and reputedly was part of an unsuccessful plot to assassinate the Kaiser, which was only aborted at the last minute when Wilhelm had to cancel a trip to Düsseldorf owing to a demonic bout of haemorrhoids. Dolby was born in Agra, and moved from Stamford Bridge to Brentford.

Another illustrious amateur, Max Woosnam, also pulled on the Blue shirt in the 1913/14 season, if only for three outings.

In the last weeks of the season, Calderhead brought Hamilton Academicals outside-left Bobby McNeil to the Bridge (where he would remain until 1929). A teacher and Scottish international, Jimmy Croal came from Falkirk. He would be on Chelsea's books until 1922 when he went to Fulham. Initially, this Caledonian pairing were not a popular duo at the Bridge, holding up attacking movements with their subtle dribbling, but, as they became accustomed to the faster pace of the English game, the Chelsea fans took them to their collective heart.

Colin Hampton was persuaded to leave Motherwell and keep goal in the Chelsea cause and was to remain under the Blue flag for a decade, mostly playing as a reserve.

THE BIRTH OF THE BLUES

In April 1914, football and, more specifically, Chelsea were cited as being fashionable by no lesser authority than *The Times*, which declared, 'In the last two or three years, League matches at Stamford Bridge and elsewhere have been attended even by persons to whom the dangerous epithet fashionable might be applied ... Professional football of the best kind is no longer regarded as a spectacle only for the proletariat.'

Chelsea finished their 1913/14 campaign in the top half of the First Division (eighth) for the first time and it seemed as if the team were ready to make a real challenge for glory the following season.

On a sad note that season, on Monday, 27 April, the fans saw some of the great players of the time – Bob Crompton, Billy Meredith, Arthur Grimsdell and 'Fanny' Walden – come together at Stamford Bridge for a North vs. South testimonial game for Ben Warren, Chelsea's former wing-half whose career had ended while he was at the peak of his game. He had been plagued with sickness and depression and his is perhaps the most tragic story of Chelsea's first few years.

Money raised from Warren's testimonial match would help support his wife and children. Almost 12,000 turned up in the spring sunshine to support Ben, and the display of skill from the likes of Viv Woodward made for an entertaining game.

Born in 1880, at Newhall, near Burton, Derbyshire, right-half Warren had come to Stamford Bridge from Derby County in 1908 at the age of 28. During his four years with Chelsea, he was a habitual goalscorer. He was known for his elegant play and consistency but also as a kind and courageous man with a tremendous sense of sportsmanship that was recognised throughout the game.

After getting a kick in the stomach in December 1909, Warren developed a cyst that had to be removed by surgery. He then picked up a head injury, which numbered him among the long list of casualties that motivated the club to unsuccessfully attempt to buy the means to keep them in the First Division.

Warren shone in the Second Division; however, in October 1911, during Chelsea's promotion season, Ben picked up a serious knee injury, which, along with the loss of earnings, with a young family to support, caused him tremendous anxiety. In those days, before national insurance, footballers, like most other workers, did not receive sick pay. The cost was a mental and physical breakdown that resulted in his never again playing football.

Over the short period of two months, Warren became prone to odd behaviour and occasional violence. He was admitted to a private clinic in Nottingham, the Coppice, on 15 December, with what was then described as 'acute mania'.

In February 1912, Warren was admitted to the Derby County Lunatic Asylum at Mickleover, where his case notes reveal he suffered a rapid decline in his physical and mental health. He would spend five years at Mickleover until his death on 15 January 1917. An England international footballer, Ben Warren was buried as a 'pauper' at the age of 37.

15
THE GOOD,
THE BAD AND
THE LUCKY

Our number-one opponents are not Liverpool, Arsenal or
Manchester United. It is ourselves at Chelsea.

Didier Drogba (Chelsea, 2004 – present)

1914/15

It was a confusing task playing professional
football during the opening months of World War
I, with as many people approving as disapproving
of being paid to play a game while the country
prepared to defend itself from the threat of the
enemy. But of all the clubs that could possibly
divert people just a little from the frightening and
dramatic consequences of European conflict,
Chelsea proved the most likely when they, in the

true spirit of contradiction, 'did the double'; of making it to their first FA Cup Final and getting themselves relegated from the First Division for the second time in their decade of history.

The end of October saw Chelsea without a League win but this time the Pensioners were unable to find a way out and the cruel sword of destiny fell in the last game of the term; a 2–0 defeat at Meadow Lane by fellow bottom dwellers Notts County. It was a bad day for London as Spurs finished last, just one point behind the Bridge boys.

Initially in the Cup, the West Londoners' fortunes looked little better than their League prospects. After the first-round 1–1 draw with Swindon Town at the Bridge, it seemed to be business as usual in terms of the great English Cup for Chelsea. And this appeared more than confirmed in the replay (also contested in SW6 by mutual agreement) when the West Country team were leading by 2–1 with normal time running out. But 'Happy' Harry Ford equalised for the Pensioners to send the match into extra-time in which Chelsea hit three goals to run out 5–2 winners. During this era it was normal that drawn

Cup ties after 90 minutes' play would go to a second replay. But regulations that had been introduced for wartime conditions forbade games to be played on any other day than Saturday and stipulated that Cup replays should be settled by half an hour of extra-time.

The second round brought Chelsea up against then Second Division Woolwich Arsenal, in their first season at Highbury. A goal from Harold Halse sent the glum Gunners back to North London as losers. Bob Thomson scored the only goal of the away game with Manchester City, who were second in the League at that point in the season and this was followed by a 1–1 draw with five-times finalists Newcastle United at the Bridge. Once more it was Thomson who was the man on target for the Pensioners. This took Chelsea to St James' Park where the only goal of the game (scored by Harry Ford) put them in the last four where they would face Everton, the side that would win the League that season, at Villa Park.

Everton were four-times Cup finalists and had won the trophy in 1906, which made them among the best performers in the First Division in the old knockout competition. Chelsea did well to hold the

Toffees' attack in an even first half. Goals by way of Jimmy Croal and a brilliant solo effort by Halse, with no reply from Everton, took the Pensioners to their first major Final and their last 'official' one up to 1967 (as wartime trophies were not considered to be 'official').

Although the 44th FA Cup Final was to be somewhat anti-climactic for Chelsea, in that it was a dismally unbalanced match in which the Londoners were effectively outclassed by Sheffield United, this should not detract from Chelsea's achievement of reaching the Final of what was then the most competitive and high-quality football competition in the world. It was a fantastic feat after just 10 years in existence to have made the Final of the premier football competition in the world. No other club in the professional era could claim such success and the Pensioners did make a fight of it against a team that would finish 13 places and 14 points above them in the League.

Those with any involvement with Chelsea past, present or future would be unfair to disparage David Calderhead's team and belittle the mountain they climbed, especially in a period when the feeling that the usual football structure should be abandoned was growing apace in the light of the carnage the War was threatening. Crowds were dwindling because of the demands of the armed forces, war-work and simple discomfort about watching a game while Britain was defending itself against a dangerous and close-at-hand enemy.

With the War already eight months old and teams decimated by players being taken away on more urgent matters, the venue of the Final, with security in mind, was switched from Crystal Palace to Old Trafford. This meant that Chelsea lost something of a 'natural' geographical advantage that they would have had playing at Crystal Palace, while their opponents Sheffield United could only have benefited from the change.

This was not a time when travelling all over the country was easy and few West London fans were able to make the journey to Manchester on 24 April 1915. Those who did make the trek 'up North' for the Final had to deal with the rail services operating under wartime restrictions.

So it was Sheffield United supporters that made up the majority of the close to 50,000 spectators that watched the one-sided encounter. According to the *Manchester Guardian*, the crowd 'included numbers of men in uniform ... In the lower rows of the stand there was a group of wounded soldiers, accompanied by their nurses. Several of them had their feet in bandages and one, minus an arm, smoked his pipe and viewed the game in an air of perfect contentment. There was never a Cup Final played in such a depressing atmosphere. A sombre consciousness of war overhung the crowd, and the final touch was when the band started to play hymns.'

Lt VJ Woodward was granted special leave from France for the game and travelled from the front to Old Trafford. He had been one of the first players in the Football League to volunteer for the 17th Battalion of the Middlesex Regiment. This was one of what were known as the 'Pals' battalions formed during the early stages of World War I. The epithet of the 'Footballers Battalion' would become legendary and it included many of Woodward's former teammates from his days with Spurs. He served on the Western Front and was wounded in 1916. He eventually reached the rank of captain.

THE BIRTH OF THE BLUES

The War meant that Woodward's playing career at Chelsea had virtually ended, but after the conflict he became a director of the club. In a letter from France, he had underlined that none of his teammates who had taken Chelsea to their first Final should be displaced. So, for purely sporting and gentlemanly reasons, and despite the pleas of the Chelsea manager and board, he refused to take over from Bob Thomson, who had won a regular place in the Pensioners' attack. Thomson had played in every round of the Cup and was his side's top scorer in the competition, having hit six goals on the way to Old Trafford. But there was little doubt that, deprived of Woodward's inspirational leadership and graceful running, Chelsea were the poorer.

In the rather artificial ambience, Chelsea took to the field in unfamiliar white shirts on a sunless, grey day that had threatened at one point to thicken to a yellowish fog and force a stoppage or even the abandonment of the Final. As it was, it rained from the start of the match to the final whistle. With the crowd predominantly in khaki (the event came to be remembered as 'The Khaki Final') and the War looming over events like a dark spectre, it was a strange time, place and atmosphere for a Cup Final.

The Final teams were:

SHEFFIELD UNITED: Harold Gough; Bill Cook, Jack English, Albert Sturgess, Bill Brelsford, George Utley, Jim Simmons, Stan Fazackerley, Joe Kitchen, Wally Masterman, Bobby Evans

CHELSEA: Jim Molyneux; Wally Bettridge, Jack Harrow, Fred Taylor, Tom Logan, Andrew Walker, Harry Ford, Harold Halse, Bob Thomson, Jim Croal, Bob McNeil

Chelsea's first FA Cup Final would not exactly prove to be the pinnacle of their initial decade of history and it has often been portrayed as a bad memory for the club.

Compared to their opponents, Sheffield United had a relatively easy path to the Final (far less mileage and playing six games while the Londoners had been through seven matches), seeing off fellow Northerners Blackpool, Liverpool, Bradford, Oldham Athletic (after a replay) on their way to a semi-final encounter with Bolton Wanderers (who would finish the season just one point clear of relegation) at Ewood Park. The Blades had scored nine goals (of which Kitchen had hit four) on their way to Old Trafford compared to the 12 the Pensioners had netted, but the Yorkshiremen's defence had been breached on only two occasions, whereas Chelsea had let in four.

One writer claimed that Sheffield brushed Chelsea away 'as if they were novices', and the Blades did have a fine half-back line that did a good job for them on the day, with George Utley doing exceptionally well. But let's be clear what kind of side Chelsea were facing. The Blades were one of the most successful of the time. They had been established since 1889, over a quarter of a century, more than twice the time Chelsea had been around. They had been well set from the start at Bramall Lane (the oldest major ground anywhere in the world).

Sheffield United had been Football League Champions in 1898 and runners-up in 1897 and 1900, and they had won the FA Cup in 1899 and 1902. They were beaten finalists in 1901 and had finished second in Division Two in 1893. United had produced Ernest Needham, William Foulke and Billy Hendry in their early years and before 1920 the likes of Alf Common, Albert Sturgess and George Utley had emerged as all-time great Blades; their Cup Final side boasted four England internationals in Gough, Sturgess, Utley and Evans.

The nearest that one might come to imagining a Final with contemporary equivalents in terms of relative success and tradition might be a Wembley confrontation between AFC Wimbledon and Everton.

However, it is true that Harry Ford (who was carrying an injury) hardly managed to get a kick of the ball and that Brelsford, not the biggest centre-half around and maybe not even among the tallest of the shortest in the top flight, was too powerful for the diminutive Bob Thompson. Thompson was not fully recovered from a dislocated elbow that had given him trouble during his rare rampages down the middle and even his courage could not compensate for this injury.

The *Manchester Guardian* told a sorry tale for the Londoners: 'Chelsea only got in two really good shots and those came in the last few seconds of the first half. They were hard ground shots to the foot of the post and came so quickly that Gough had only just time to rush from the one post to the other.

'At the beginning of the second half the fog was so dense that spectators on the one side had only the haziest notion of what was happening on the other, and the ball was rarely seen except when it rose against the sky.'

For most of the Final, the Pensioners were under constant pressure from a fired-up Blades attack that caused even the usually calm Walter Bettridge to lose his poise at times.

The playing conditions were bad and so was the morale and attitude of the London side in what was considered to be the last peacetime FA Cup Final for five years (as it was the last to be run in the conventional nationally contested fashion until the 1919/20 season – there were 'wartime' cups run on a regional basis but none was for the FA Cup). Throughout most of the match, mistakes were made constantly by the beleaguered Pensioners. Just 36 minutes after Mr HH Taylor of Altrincham had blown his whistle to start, confusion in the Chelsea defence led to Sheffield

United taking the lead. An error by Harrow, who between 1911 and 1926 would become the first Chelsea player to play over 300 games (333 in all, scoring five goals), and a fumble by the keeper allowed United their first goal. Simmons had beaten two defenders before smashing the ball beyond Jim Molyneux. With the whole of the Sheffield side now storming the Blue ramparts, Chelsea did well to hold them off for most of what remained of the match. But goals from Utley and predictably Kitchen in the last six minutes effectively settled issues.

JAH Catton, the famous sports writer of the day, was to tell how 'Chelsea were as helpless as a reed shaken in the wind. They would not have scored had they played for a week.'

But between themselves the press hacks seemed to have made up their minds about the character of the match, and most neglected to give credit to the Londoners, who, although having not played as well as they might, had never given up the ghost. Indeed, the match could easily have ended up as an untidy 1–0 victory for the Northerners. But perhaps, much later, Jim Molyneux's view of the game might act as something of a balance in terms of the historical view of events: 'Chelsea just didn't connect up. No player did anything wrong or even played that badly. But Sheffield were very much on form and managed to split Chelsea up into departments; divide and rule it was. We weren't far from giving them a match and if it had been possible to pull level to one apiece that day might have turned out very differently. But for us just to get to the Final was a wonderful thing. It was a proud day for us all. We'd been brought together from everywhere; a raggle-taggle army, but we never gave in!'

At the end, as the players lined up for their medals, Lord Derby declared, 'You have played well with one another and against one another. Play with one another for England now.'

Harry Wilding took his Lordship's advice and made the trip to the recruiting office; he would be awarded the Military Medal with the Grenadier Guards.

During the very odd last so-called 'peacetime' season, Jim Molyneux was once more the regular goalkeeper, with Walter Bettridge and Jack Marrow in front of him. At centre-half, Tommy Logan was usually flanked by Fred Taylor and

Laurence Abrams (although Andy Walker took his place in the FA Cup Final) who had joined the Pensioners from Heart of Midlothian. The inside-forwards were Harold Halse and Jimmy Croal, while the wingers were the swift pair of Harry Ford and Bobby McNeil (who between 1914 and 1927 would record the second-highest number of appearances for the club to that point – 307, scoring 32 times). As Vivian Woodward was serving in the army in France, Bob Thomson led the attack.

Four days after the Cup Final, defeat against Notts County realistically consigned Chelsea to the Second Division. But the Pensioners would continue to be the kings of contradiction. When hostilities ended, the Football League decided to enlarge the First Division from 20 to 22 clubs, which gave Chelsea the chance, although by no means a guarantee, to re-enter the First Division via this convenient back door. However, in December 1915, a Football League inquiry concluded that the game on the previous Good Friday involving Manchester United and Liverpool had been fixed; United had won the match 2–0, which meant they finished one point and one place above Chelsea. But the Football League believed that United had been the victim of an act by one individual and as such took no action against the club. However, huge public sympathy was expressed for Chelsea and, after the club decided to stay loyal to the Football League following the threat of a London breakaway, the Pensioners were rewarded by being elected to return to Division One. Chelsea were elevated without kicking a ball and became one of the few clubs to be relegated from Division One to continue to play in that League (at the end of the 1991/92 season, Luton Town, Notts County and West Ham United would be relegated from Division One into Division One as the Premier League came into being in 1992/93).

Protests against the continuation of professional League football in wartime finally saw the peacetime structures put into mothballs at the conclusion of the 1914/15 season. It would be four long and bloody years until the traditional structure of the game was resuscitated.

David Calderhead remained Chelsea's manager until he retired in 1933. By the end of his career, he had steered the Blues to promotion (in 1912 and

1930) and two relegations. But he guided Chelsea to
the club's first-ever FA Cup Final in 1915 and the last
four of the competition on three other occasions. His
son, David Junior, played for the Blues from 1910 to
1913, making 43 first-team appearances.

Given the relatively huge sums of money
Calderhead was provided with, it might be argued
that he could or should have achieved more and
that under his management Chelsea could only be
relied upon to be inconsistent. But his teams were
almost always entertaining and the 'Chelsea
Sphinx' was held in high regard throughout
football; few managers in the history of the
English game have come anywhere near equalling
his 26 years of service to a single club.

During July 1915, the Football League made all
players amateurs, allowing their only payment to
be expenses for tea and refreshments. Attendances
were falling and in September the game became
regional to restrict rail travel and save fuel; the
London Combination League was born out of this
situation and probably saved most of the capital's
professional clubs from ruin.

The only known fatality suffered by a former
member of the Chelsea squad as a direct result of

the conflict was Bob 'Pom Pom' Whiting, a sad irony was that he was nicknamed after slang (at the time) for a military weapon, a small machine cannon, the 'Maxim' which was first converted for light artillery use during the Boer War (1899–1902). The weapon weighed a hefty 70lb and, for the sections of the Chelsea crowd with army service, it seemed to be a suitable soubriquet for Bob as he had the ability, from the toe of his boot, to launch the ball tremendous distances. This, for many, was reminiscent of the Maxim's rapid-fire, one-pound percussion-fused shells, as a barrage was laid down on enemy lines. These were the days of Empire, when military experience was common and conflict was a constant fact of life, although not on Britain's European doorstep.

In 1906, Bob had filled the huge space left by Willie Foulke, but, weighing in at 14 stone, Whiting covered plenty of the goal-line himself. He came to Stamford Bridge from Tunbridge Wells Rangers, and missed only one game during Chelsea's promotion season of 1906/07, letting in just 34 goals in 38 matches.

The following term, Jack Whitley got the nod over Bob and he eventually joined Brighton and

Hove Albion where he won a Southern League Championship medal in 1910. At that time there was a tradition of staging a Charity Shield play-off between the Southern League Champions and the Football League Champions and on 5 September 1910 the ex-Chelsea keeper returned to Stamford Bridge to face Aston Villa in front of a crowd of 15,000. The Seagulls headed back to the coast 1–0 victors.

Whiting (like Viv Woodward) volunteered for the 17th Middlesex Regiment, the 'Football Battalion', as a private. He was killed on 28 April 1917 in the Arras offensive, near Pas de Calais, where he is buried in the Arras Memorial Cemetery. He was 34 years of age.

Although all the rest of the Chelsea players who went to war came home, some brought more back with them than others. After hostilities ended, Harry Wilding returned to the football field with shrapnel beneath his heart and Andy Wilson, who came to Chelsea after the War, had a permanently damaged arm, the result of shell fragments. In the late 1920s, following an injury in training, X-rays revealed that he was still carrying around a chunk of metal and required surgery to remove it.

But the conflict had caused maladies that X-rays could not find. On 18 August 1924, Tommy Meehan died in St George's Hospital as the result of a rare inflammation of the brain caused by a viral infection known as encephalitis lethargica, which causes mental and physical deterioration, not unlike the later stages of Parkinson's disease. Such an affliction is awful at any age but, for Tommy, a fit and active man, who was just 28 when he died, it must have been horrific. The likely cause was a worldwide epidemic of the condition that occurred between 1917 and 1928, possibly as a consequence of the massive troop and refugee movements that took place during the war years.

In 1922, *Jack's Paper*, a magazine-type journal aimed at young men, had devoted space to Tommy 'The Terrier' Meehan, calling him the 'mighty atom' and declared that he was worth his weight in gold. The journal trumpeted, 'They call Tommy a terrier – some forwards have used stronger language. He's a full 90-minute man, on the go from whistle to whistle, and there's nothing he likes more than to see two big, hefty forwards standing in the opposite line-up. He worries 'em, confuses 'em, until their nerves and skill are torn to shreds.'

Meehan was an elegant and intelligent player, a determined and creative performer in the left midfield, or working as a wing-half, and he often took the responsibility of firing penalties. He didn't drink or smoke, both uncommon abstinences among professional footballers of his day. He had turned out for Rochdale during the War. Tommy moved from Manchester United to Stamford Bridge in December 1920 for the big fee of £3,300 and the following year – alongside Nils Middelboe, David Cameron, John Priestley, Harry Wilding and intermittently Stephen Smith – he was part of a Chelsea midfield that was seen as good as any and better than many in the Football League.

CONCLUSION

*The more time you have, the more mistakes
you will make.*

Ruud Gullit (Chelsea, 1995–98)

Harry Ford's runners-up medal from the 1915 FA Cup Final was pawned after he retired from football. However, Harry's daughter was later to tell of something she still had from that game: 'We've got a programme made of silk from the 1915 Final from when he was presented to King George V. Only the players and staff got it – you couldn't buy it.'

The celebrated writer LP Hartley wrote at the start of one of his greatest stories *The Go-Between,*

'The past is a foreign country. They do things differently there...' and certainly times have changed from when players were obliged to sell items like FA Cup medals, leaving their children with only 'chance' mementoes of their proudest days while their former clubs continued to pay their shareholders dividends on their one-off purchase of shares. But the overarching ethos of Chelsea Football Club, as an organisation, has not so much changed as developed.

After the passing of Gus Mears in 1912, Chelsea changed their shirt colours to a darker blue and replaced the formerly white 'knickers' with shorts to match the new shirts. This shade of blue had come to be associated with capitalism and was the same hue as the 'blue flag' that was on occasion hoisted in certain quarters in symbolic opposition to the red flag of socialism.

Just two short years away from the Great War was a time when worker and union movements were exerting themselves. During January 1911, in East London, the Siege of Sidney Street had been fought out, with the Metropolitan Police and the Scots Guards engaging in a battle with Latvian anarchists. The British Socialist Party was founded in Manchester in that same year. The following October the British Seafarers' Union was formed in Southampton and in the winter of 1912 the 'Bread and Roses' strike took place in Lawrence, Massachusetts, an heroic action wherein more than 20,000 immigrant textile workers protested against inhuman working and living conditions. As such, in the early months of 1912, many in the entrepreneurial class began to feel somewhat uneasy, having never really experienced such a depth of mass questioning or social reaction to their activities.

Chelsea, more than any other professional club, had its roots in the making of profit; in effect, it had arisen out of that aim and the team had been conceived in the 'spirit of capitalism'. All the Pensioners' rivals by this time were also first and foremost engaged in commercial enterprise, but mostly their foundations had been primarily set in the playing of the game for its own sake, although for some the initiation of football also had other aims, not least offering institutional affiliations (in commerce and religion for example) as an alternative to union or class fidelities. But Stamford Bridge had been 'made for rent' and unlike many of its competitors it did that a lot.

The formative years of Chelsea FC seemed for some to be a time when the strength of capitalism needed to be asserted in the face of growing resistance to its excesses. The Victorian era was over, and a new world was being born wherein Britain was beginning to feel threatened by industrial competition from abroad that previously the Empire had insulated the country from. The great inland docks had been built in London over the previous hundred years and the City was burgeoning as a financial centre at the hub of a monolithic, yet still not fully mature, capitalist matrix that by its innate mechanisms pushed labour exploitation to its very limits. In some areas, this fired thoughts of revolution (early in 1919 the Seattle General Strike had been portrayed as a Communist-inspired event) but in the main the great push of capitalist endeavour existed on the cusp of worker unrest. One example of this was the 1919 national railway strike, one act within a huge wave of national unrest that year that included strikes or the threat of strikes in the docks and among other transport workers. There was a nationwide bakers strike and a rent strike by council tenants in Glasgow. Violent incidents broke out all over the country (in Glasgow the police charged 'mobs' of strikers and headlines declared 'GLASGOW BOLSHEVISM', 'DISGRACEFUL SCENES', 'RIOT ACT READ'). The press, fearing a replication of what had happened in Russia just a couple of years earlier, screamed that a 'Bolshevik revolution' was taking place in Britain.

As the rail strike began to hit home in London and hurt the employers, the buses failed to cope as commuters literally fought to board them and the capital came to a standstill. This not only threatened the profits of the railway owners, but also the trading houses of the City and so the whole British economy. As the action continued in October, the great steel strike in America was also getting under way. If the railwaymen in the UK were seen to win a massive victory by striking a telling blow to international trade, it would stand as a glowing example to workers worldwide of their power to undermine those who, through low wages and poor conditions, exploited them and their families. For many, the very idea of such a consciousness spreading threatened to realise Marxist predictions of international revolution.

The Mears family threw their weight squarely behind their class peers and JT Mears, a director of Chelsea Football Club at the time, hitting back for capitalism, sent his pleasure steamers into the heart of central London, where they landed at Westminster Pier. The initial three boats were crowded and the first four moved over 800 people into the City from Richmond, stopping at Hammersmith and Putney. The cost for the passengers was a hefty 2s 6d return, about 1d a mile.

It has become a convention for opposing fans over the years to serenade Chelsea supporters with a song that includes the instruction to stick their blue flag up their collective arse. Ironically, this is traditionally sung to the melody of the international socialist anthem 'The Red Flag'.

Chelsea were founded and sustained by men totally committed to profit and who revered business ethics. As such, Chelsea have always been the football club that have led the way in the transformation of the game into a commercial enterprise. The modern incarnation of the club is founded on wealth arising out of the eruption of the pugnacious and primitive capitalism in Russia and as such keeps faith with the very roots of the club. If you want to see the way football is going, look to Chelsea. It is a team based in England, but with an international profile that would look more at home in a world league alongside AC Milan, Manchester United, Boca Juniors and Barcelona than in the Premiership populated with the likes of Wigan and where teams such as Portsmouth (with its 20,000-capacity ground) boast a place in the top rank.

Chelsea Football Club have indeed come a long way, but in essence they have stayed true to their colours. The team started out to draw in their fans by means of entertaining and star-studded teams who were capable of achieving good results quickly.

In the contemporary era, success and entertainment is all, whether on television or in music or sport. Today, crowds will not come to Old Trafford, The Emirates or Stamford Bridge to watch 'interesting' games, and it is no longer our priority to see 'the ball on the ground' or the most skilful of play. All that, along with the notion of 'loyalty to the shirt', is gravy, for, first and foremost, a team must win, and if this is done via bland 'route one' tactics, and/or continued diving and play acting, so be it; the aesthetic of the game has been sacrificed to market forces wherein the highest commodity is victory.

At school, when I was about 9 or 10, the teacher who ran the football team once told us, 'Football is all about winning.' I wasn't convinced by that statement then and I am even less persuaded by it now. Football, as a social thing, is about celebrating wins and dealing with losses; it is about fidelity, identity and solidarity. The great Celtic manager Jock Stein, a miner and the son of a miner, argued that football is a 'type of socialism', while his footballing contemporary Bill Shankly, the legendary manager of Liverpool, declared, 'The socialism I believe in is everyone working for each other, everyone having a share of the rewards. It's the way I see football, the way I see life.'

In the hardest times for the club, Chelsea fans would have recognised and I think agreed (like most true football supporters) with this sentiment. It is that which has supplied the team with their continued support and will keep them relevant and pertinent in the future. Without support, football is nothing at all, a mere game mostly played by men who might struggle with the everyday challenges that those who support them accept and deal with one after the other. They may come to the Bridge for every game, wear the shirt or just make the results they achieve the first thing they look at in the newspaper or on the internet. These people cannot be bought and sold, but are the only real value of the game; they are born to be Blue and it is they who have made Chelsea's history and will provide it with a future.

CHELSEA TIMELINE

1873 Lillie Bridge, home of the London Athletic Club (LAC) from 1869 to 1877, hosts the FA Cup Final.

Henry Augustus (Gus) Mears is born.

1877 Brothers James and William Waddell purchase land on behalf of the LAC where they build a stadium. On 28 April, the original Stamford Bridge ground opens as an athletics venue.

1880 The Underground District Line extension to Putney Bridge, taking in Walham Green, is laid.

1888 Lillie Bridge ground closes.

1896 Gus has the idea of making Stamford Bridge a top football venue.

1898 Stamford Bridge hosts the World Shinty Championship.

FEBRUARY 1904 At the annual meeting of the LAC, the club committee proclaims that the club are seeking new accommodation and their former ground is to be handed over to Mears on 24 June. Mears provides assurances that the LAC will be able to continue using the stadium.

29 SEPTEMBER 1904 The freehold of Stamford Bridge is transferred to Gus Mears.

1905 Negotiations with Fulham for the lease of Stamford Bridge break down. Frederick Parker meet Gus Mears at Stamford Bridge where Mears's dog Bluey bites Parker.

FEBRUARY 1905 Gus Mears recruits the Scottish architect Archibald Leitch, the legendary

'Engineering Archie', to design a new East Stand as the centrepiece of Stamford Bridge.

14 MARCH 1905 The first meeting of the new football club takes place at The Rising Sun pub; one of the first decisions is to name the club Chelsea.

27 MARCH 1905 John Tait Robertson is named as Chelsea's player/secretary-manager.

29 MAY 1905 At a meeting at the Tavistock Hotel, Covent Garden Plaza, London, Chelsea are admitted to the Football League.

1 JUNE 1905 Chelsea's inaugural board meeting as a Football League club takes place.

2 SEPTEMBER 1905 Chelsea lose their first competitive match away to Stockport County in Division Two 1–0.

4 SEPTEMBER 1905 Gus Mears kicks off Chelsea's first game at Stamford Bridge, a friendly against Liverpool.

13 SEPTEMBER 1905 Player/secretary-manager Jock Robertson scores Chelsea's first League goal in their League debut game at Stamford Bridge vs. Hull City. It is also the club's first League win.

MARCH 1906 Stamford Bridge hosts the Football League vs. The Scottish League.

APRIL 1906 Chelsea finish third in Division Two.

MAY 1906 George 'Gatling Gun' Hilsdon moves from Upton Park to Stamford Bridge.

27 NOVEMBER 1906 John Tait Robertson resigns.

16 FEBRUARY 1907 George Hilsdon become the first Chelsea player to be capped for England playing for the English League side.

27 APRIL 1907 Chelsea finish as runners-up in Division Two and are promoted to Division One.

AUGUST 1907 David Calderhead takes over as Chelsea's secretary-manager.

THE BIRTH OF THE BLUES

7 SEPTEMBER 1907 Chelsea play their first Division One game vs. Sheffield United at Stamford Bridge; the Blades win 4–2.

1909 Vivian Woodward joins Chelsea.

Full-back Jack Cameron becomes Chelsea's first Scottish international player when he is selected for the side to meet England.

27 DECEMBER 1909 70,000, the largest ever attendance at an English League game, come to Stamford Bridge to see Newcastle United defeated.

13 APRIL 1910 Chelsea are relegated from Division One.

14 JANUARY 1911 Chelsea reach the FA Cup semi-final for the first time.

11 MARCH 1911 Swindon Town, then a Southern League side, are beaten 3–1 at the Bridge in the quarter-final of the FA Cup; the record 77,952 crowd is the highest attendance for any FA Cup tie outside the Final to that date.

29 APRIL 1911 Chelsea finish third in Division Two, two points behind promoted Bolton.

4 FEBRUARY 1912 Gus Mears dies.

29 APRIL 1912 Chelsea finish second in Division Two and are promoted.

1913 Tom Hewitt plays three times for Wales in all their Home International games. He will be the last Chelsea man to win a Welsh cap until 1963 when Graham Moore is selected for the side to play Brazil.

5 APRIL 1913 England beat Scotland in the first of three pre-World War II internationals to be staged at the stadium watched by a crowd of 52,000.

26 FEBRUARY 1914 The New York Giants play the Chicago White Sox at Stamford Bridge as the finale of their 1913/14 World Tour.

24 APRIL 1915 Chelsea meet Sheffield United at Old Trafford in the Blues' first FA Cup Final.

BIBLIOGRAPHY

I have made reference to a number of texts to illuminate statistics, facts, individual player details and match reports. I have also called on many other national newspapers, club histories and Who's Who publications relating to other clubs. Autobiographies and biographies of other players and managers have informed the work as have football reference books used to confirm details.

As in most historic research, one comes across contradictory information. In some cases, I have been obliged to make judgements about what is most probable, given the contextual information.

Benson, C. (1987) *The Bridge* Commodore

Cheshire, S. (1991) *Chelsea. A Complete Record*
Breedon

Cheshire, S. (1994) *Chelsea – An Illustrated
History* Breedon

Cheshire, S. (2003) *The Legends of Chelsea* Breedon

Cheshire, S. & Hockings, R. (1986) *Chelsea
Football Club. The Full Statistical Story*
Ron Hockings

Cheshire, S. & Hockings, R. (1987) *Chelsea FC
Players Who's Who* Scott Cheshire

Farror, M. & Lamming, D. (1972) *A Century of
English International Football: 1872–1972*
Robert Hale

Finn, R. (1969) *A History of Chelsea F.C.*
Sportsman's Book Club

Glanvill, R. (2005) *Chelsea F.C. The Official
Biography* Headline

Goldsworthy, M. (1969) *The Encyclopaedia of
Association Football* Robert Hale and Co.

Goldsworthy, M. (1972) *We Are the Champions:
A History of the Football League Champions
1888–1972* Pelham Books

Groves. R. (1947) *Chelsea* Famous
Football Clubs

Harris, H. (2005) *Chelsea Century* John Blake

Harrison, P. (2005) *The Stamford Bridge Encyclopedia* Mainstream

Henderson, N. (1998) *Chelsea Feeling Blue* The People's History

Lane, D. (2003) *Stamford Bridge Legends* Legends

Lerman, R. & Brown, D. (1998) *The Blues. Day-to-Day Life at Stamford Bridge* Mainstream

Lovering, P. (1993) *Chelsea; Player by Player* Hamlyn

Matthew, T. (2005) *Who's Who of Chelsea* Mainstream

Mears, B. & Macleay, I. (2001) *Chelsea. Football Under the Blue Flag* Mainstream

Mears, B. & Macleay, I. (2005) *Chelsea. The 100-Year History* Mainstream

Moynihan, J. (1982) *The Chelsea Story* Arthur Barker

Moynihan, L. (2005) *Chelsea's Cult Heroes* Know How to Score

Pickard, A. & W. (1905–06) *Association Football and the Men Who Made It* (4 vols) Caxton Publishing Company

Prole, D. (1964) *Football in London* Robert Hale

Phythian, G. (2005) *Colossus – The True Story of William Foulke* Tempus

Sewell, A. (Ed) (1970 to 1974) *The Chelsea Football Book Nos 1–5* Stanley Paul

JOURNALS/NEWSPAPERS

Athletic News
Football Chat
Fulham Chronicle
Jack's Paper
Manchester Guardian
The Times
West London & Fulham Times

OTHER PUBLICATIONS

Chelsea Chronicles and matchday programmes 1905–2008 Chelsea FC handbooks and yearbooks 1905–2008

F.A. Book for Boys Match, Shoot!, Topical Times annuals

Association of Football Statisticians (AFS) Bulletin (various)

ARCHIVES ETC.

1837online.com

Archive General de la Nacion. Argentina

British Library

British Library Newspapers

British Pathe

Derbyshire Records Office

Guildhall Library

Greater Manchester Records Office

Hammersmith and Fulham Archives and Family
History Centre

University of Leicester

London Metropolitan Archives

National Football Museum, Preston

Westminster Libraries